<u>Money...</u>
It's Not Just
for Rich
People!

A Ridiculously Simple Path to Wealth Accumulation

Janine Bolon

The stories and anecdotes described in this book are based on personal experiences of the author and her clients. Most of the names are pseudonyms, and some situations have been modified slightly for educational purposes and to protect the individuals' privacy. This book is not designed to provide specific legal, investment, or accounting advice or any professional service by its publication. Each individual's situation is unique, so specific financial questions should be addressed to a suitable professional. The Author and Publisher specifically disclaim any liability that is incurred from the use or application of the contents of this book.

Visit our website at www.smartcentsinc.com

Cover Design by David Glenn

Published by SmartCents,Inc.

First edition published 2005

This work is dedicated to

my mother,

Saundra Dalziel,

who gave me wings

and to my guru,

Paramahansa Yogananda,

who taught me to fly.

Acknowledgements

The one person that I most wish to thank is my dear friend and husband, Dr. Brad Bolon. Without his unflagging support with funding, child care, house work, editorial assistance, and general advice, this project would never have come to pass.

My sister, Bonnie Komenda, needs to be recognized for her guidance on the different models of enterprise. Her advice influenced how I have structured my current successful business in financial education.

I commend my father, Douglas Dalziel, for being an invaluable teacher in the art of human behavior and for my heritage from him of a "golden Irish tongue."

I extend my thanks to Dr. Julie Earl for her patient listening and strength of experience as the seminar that culminated in this book was first discussed and organized. Her suggestions on delivery, timing, and story telling were quite valuable.

I am grateful to all the people who participated in this study for their willingness to open their financial lives to my prying questions and comments. Even with anonymity it is not easy for us to reveal past mistakes or open emotional wounds, but all of them did so with honesty and frankness. I am honored to have had the opportunity to work with every one of them. Their courage and strength of commitment to financial well being is truly inspiring.

Thank you, Josef Komenda, my long time friend and computer geek, who helped me navigate the wondrous world of Lulu Enterprises publishing.

Finally, to Dr. Oliver DeMille and Mrs. Rachel DeMille, thank you for spreading the word about this project, for believing in me when no one had heard me discuss this topic before, and for lending your individual cachet to its success.

J.B.

Cedar City, UT
August 2005

Forward

Thank you, dear reader, for buying this book. I wanted to warn you before you got too far into it that this work is the combined outcome of my thesis research for a Master of Arts degree in Education and the begging and pleading of my clients to compile all this information into an easily accessible and always available book. After my seminars and classes, I would get constant requests for copies of my thesis results! An unheard of thing in the academic world, to have people actually wanting to *read* a thesis! Knowing the speed of the publication process for trade books (a three-toed sloth looks fast in comparison), I realized that folks would have to wait years before the "real" book was printed. There was so much more work to be done, facts to consider, and people to interview.

However, your cries were not in vain. This document should tide you over. It merges the principles and data from my research as well as the experiences of myself and others to provide you with a simple routine of daily activities that you can perform to work toward your financial independence.

I know you will find this product helpful. And stay tuned … more is coming.

Table of Contents

My Guinea Pigs

America, both its individual citizens and its local and national governments, is awash in debt. Individually and collectively, we are on a path to financial slavery. I know that this crisis can be changed through education. The object of this work was to test one potential solution.

The major goal of my experiment was to determine whether or not the habits needed for successful wealth accumulation could be instilled in individuals by a brief educational forum followed by three months of telephone mentoring. My hypothesis was that a short but good fiscal education based on universal principles would motivate almost anyone to *get started now*. Success was defined as a seminar participant who was able to increase his or her savings by at least 10% over the three months of the study. The balance in long-term savings accounts (individual retirement accounts [IRAs] and 401ks) was chosen as the test indicator for wealth-accumulating tendencies because contributions to such vehicles cannot be withdrawn easily for use in short-term consumption and thus represent a real measure of wealth building for one's future.

The initial study population consisted of 135 participants who attended a financial independence seminar that I gave in November, 2004 at George Wythe College, Cedar City, UT. [George Wythe College is a liberal arts institution dedicated to improving people's capacities for self and community fulfillment.] Of these participants, 113 individuals signed up for free telephone mentoring. After the first phone call, 38 people (34%) did not complete their assigned homework and were dropped from the study. The remaining 75 participants (representing 33 families and 9 single students) received two additional phone calls, and provided the data used in testing the hypothesis.

Before attending the seminar, the total balance in the average participant's savings accounts was $5,812. For 34 people (45%), the balance was $500 or less. This savings was typically held in a short-term savings account, even though (57%) of the families did have retirement accounts in place.

After completing three months of mentoring, 95% of the participants (31 of 33 families and all nine students) had adopted habits that promote long-term wealth accumulation. After attending the seminar and being mentored, the average wealth accumulator's savings account had increased to $8,609 (up by 48%), with increases recorded in both short-term and long-term savings vehicles. More importantly, the 45% of people who had saved $500 or less before the program now had savings account balances of $1,044 or more (an increase of at least 109%)! Of all the participants who had received the classroom experience and intensive follow-up coaching, only two families chose not to become wealth accumulators in the three-month period.

These data clearly demonstrate that a brief, practical educational experience regarding personal financial practices followed by short-term coaching can inspire people to develop habits that will promote wealth accumulation and, eventually, financial independence. Over 95% of the seminar participants benefited from this experience.

More importantly, these results indicate that wealth accumulation is a matter of habit. *And that means that you, too, can profit from these principles.* Money isn't just for rich people! Money is for those who want to be rich – not just in assets, but in contentment – and are willing to learn new habits to bring riches into their lives.

Introduction:

How Did This Happen?

I never had a desire to teach financial principles.

My real passion is science. I started my Master's degree in Education hoping that one day I could teach my favorite topics, Mathematics and Theoretical Physics. (Yep, I'm a card-carrying geek.) I have long dreamed of spending whole semesters describing the nature of Pi, Zero, and Probabilities to eager young minds. (Major geek!)

Okay, you can stop cringing now. I know that not everyone shares my science dream, so I'll leave that story for another day. Instead, this book is about something for which we all have passion: money, and how to wallow in it.

My recent life experiences, culminating in the thesis work for my Master's degree, have shown me that the Universe needs me and like-minded people for a very special purpose – to educate people on how our simple, everyday monetary choices lead us away from a life of grinding, debt-induced poverty to one of permanent wealth accumulation and real financial freedom.

You and I have collided in Space and Time by means of this work. Let me guess why you are reading. The reason you picked up this book is that your current financial situation is not to your liking. You either need a solution to your debt situation, advice (a swift kick in the right direction), or a totally fresh perspective on money. So far so good. But why should you listen to me? Maybe it is because the stars have decided to create a rift in the space-time sheet that holds our Universe together. You have mistakenly fallen into a Void and need a bold rescue craft to pull you out before you reach the black hole. You're probably on the event horizon and are about to be pulled into spaghetti strings unless you find a way out of your current financial dilemma.

I've Been There

Well, you're in luck. I know the way to go. I am a wealth accumulator. I started with no tangible assets two decades ago, and now my husband and I have enough so that we don't have to work. More importantly, we did this without any special talents: no extraordinary genius in investing, or ability to play professional sports, or luck in winning the lottery. No, we are financially independent because we spent those years learning the true principles of successful wealth accumulation – and then using them.

I have been teaching these universal principles for almost a decade and have seen remarkable changes in the lives of my students and clients. If you want to join the parade to financial freedom, keep reading and come along.

First, please know that my personal situation is not unique. We all face financial challenges. Ten years ago, I stumbled across some basic principles about money. It was a challenging time in my life. I am trained as a biochemist with a specialty in analytical chemistry, and had been working in the pharmaceutical industry for 15 years. Suddenly, I found myself pregnant. What? Excuse me? This was quite a shock to my husband and me. We had been married for ten years and figured the whole parenthood gig had passed us by long ago; I watched the probability of motherhood drop logarithmically with each passing year. However, the Universe had a good laugh at my expense, and reassigned me into the brand new career of stay-at-home mom.

After years of corporate life, this new "position" was challenging to say the least. My husband and I suddenly found ourselves with half the anticipated income, no friends (we had just moved to the Garden State), and to top it all off I was fearful that my brain would rot from lack of stimulation. After all, I was no longer working out the mathematics to molar solutions, nor calculating the flow rates of analytical instruments. (Science geek, remember?) Instead, I found myself calculating the number of wet diapers to soiled diapers and watching the circumference of my baby's head change as he grew. Once the shock and trauma of parenthood softened a bit (this took six months for me, even longer for my husband), I knew I had to find a job. Not outside of the home, but I had to exercise my brain before it disintegrated into something resembling my baby's rice cereal. But what?

The Beginning

One day my husband handed me a magazine article entitled "Live on $17,500 a Year." The article was about a woman with six children who lived in Maine. Her name was Amy Dacyczyn, author of *The Tightwad Gazette*. After reading about this Frugal Zealot, as her friends call her, I realized I had found my new vocation. It became my job to slash our family's expenses as low as I could without deprivation or starvation. I then read a book recommended in Amy's *Gazette* called *Your Money or Your Life*, written by Joe Dominguez and Vicki Robin. These two books became my scriptures for financial health and well being. By implementing the principles in these two books, my family saved more money then we ever had while I was working. My husband, Brad, was dumbfounded at how this could happen when our income had dropped by so much.

Cutting our expenses liberated us. Brad was offered a new job in southern California, and so we moved from our rented 900-square-foot apartment in central New Jersey to a cute 1600-square-foot town home in Ventura County. My hand shook as I signed the mortgage (our first!). Brad and I had never taken on so much debt before. As we settled into our new digs and the new job, I knew that I had all the pieces needed for frugality, but I didn't have a plan for where I was going. If corporate America taught me anything, it was how to plan for the future, to decrease risk, and to increase cash flow. I knew the type of life that we were currently living was not conducive to the overall, long-term health of my family. I wanted my husband to have the same freedom that I experienced every day as a stay-at-home mom. (Of course, he questions whether eternal child care equates to "freedom," but he agrees that autonomy to choose one's daily activities – including child care – is a big step toward enjoying a really contented life.) I wanted him out of the rat race so he could focus on what he truly loves, which is studying, teaching, and writing.

So, I hit the books again and dug even deeper into the literature on frugality and financial well being. My plan was to develop my financial wisdom to the point that my husband could retire from corporate life in 14 years (age 50 for him). We were amazed when the Universe made it happen in only seven years time – even while Brad and I received three more children and were challenged with a series of serious medical conditions.

How did we know that the universal principles I had discovered were true? Simple. We had loads of evidence that my financial planning had, quite literally, paid off. We were able to move our family to southern Utah without having jobs waiting for us. We bought a home when we got here, and paid it off in cash. We have a steady stream of money flowing into our lives from two home-based, part-time businesses. We have leisure to spend with our children, to continue our educations, and to travel.

We see ourselves as truly wealthy, and obviously it's true. We are wealthy in friends, in health, and, oh yeah, in money, too. Why? Because we have learned and consistently follow the basic financial principles by which the Universe works. We have it all – not in the sense of "lifestyles of the rich and famous," but in the manner of "lifestyles of the ordinary and contented." The best part of the equation is that **the path we followed is open to all**. It's not rocket science. However, it does require a thorough understanding of how to work with the Universal principles of financial freedom, and a deep commitment to make these concepts work in one's own life.

Why You Should Read This Book

This book is about becoming a wealth accumulator and a conserver of all your resources. It focuses on money, but the principles also apply to your time and energy as well. Why did I bother to write this book? The simplest answer is that it had to be done. As of this writing, I have read dozens of books on financial independence, wealth accumulation, frugality, and the conserver lifestyle. Of all the books I have surveyed on these topics, I have only read two that actually present one with a practical road map to making this conserver lifestyle work. In each of these books, there were certain omissions. I hope to remedy these omissions by presenting this information in a way that allows you to implement basic principles of wealth accumulation through easy-to-use systems.

No matter what your current financial situation, there are universal principles that you can employ to better your fiscal standing. If you consistently implement these principles, you will become a wealth accumulator. *You cannot fail* to improve your financial status if you correctly apply these principles. By learning how to utilize money in a conscious rather than reflexive manner, you will automatically manage your finances in a fashion that will allow you to become financially independent.

I have taken these principles to heart in my own life, and they obviously work because my family is financially independent. Indeed, I am so certain that they will work for anyone that I have started a company, SmartCents, to educate people on creating their own plans for financial independence. I am not an attorney, accountant, or a financial planner. I cannot give advice on how to spend your money or on what savings plans are best or which expenditures have the greatest tax advantages. What I can do, however, is show you that by using the right systems of money management and basic principles you will reap a financial benefit.

But first you have to make a choice. Will you commit to learning these principles? Will you decide to do the steps I outline here for you? Will you stop your habit-centered lifestyle and choose to adopt a thoughtful, frugality-centered one instead? After you say "yes" to these questions, one of the proven paths that you can follow is given in this book. All you have to do is act.

Chapter 1:
The Basics

The first thing to understand about gaining financial independence is that there are two distinct paths to achieve it. One path is sexy, and the other is methodical. The two paths are to increase your income (sexy) or to decrease your expenses and save (methodical).

The sexy way to financial independence has been trumpeted by many exceptional authors and personalities that teach you how to double your income. Interestingly, they frequently forget to mention the perils of this pathway. Stock market crashes, company bankruptcies, or corporate mergers, to name just a few. However, the primary peril we see so much today has nothing to do with the health of your employer, and everything to do with your own attitude toward money. This hazard is the "keeping up with the

Jones" dilemma. Even if you have a good salary, if you don't actually monitor your expenses, you'll end up raising your cost of living along with your income just to impress your family and friends. You'll have a rich income, but you'll be spending so much that you won't actually be accumulating any real wealth. By all means, find new ways to earn more money. Just remember that you don't become financially independent by making more money, but by keeping it.

And that is where the methodical way to financial freedom comes into play. This book focuses on the steady, reliable method of saving consistently while decreasing your burn rate (expenses). Why? Because when you save while lowering your spending, you are keeping more of your hard-earned money for yourself – and that's the most dependable means of winning this game!

This book will teach you to reduce your expenses, pay off your debt load, and establish a consistent pattern of saving. Together, these three actions will help you to accumulate real wealth. Then you will be prepared to learn how to really use your money to best effect when you do double your income.

The Five Basic Laws of Wealth Accumulation

There are five basic principles to the wealth accumulator lifestyle. These are:

Create Your Financial Goals – this gives you direction

Live Within Your Means – don't spend money you don't actually have

Pay Yourself First – save, save, save!

Pay It Forward – take care of your retirement

Philanthropy – take care of others

If you enact these five concepts in your life, your financial situation will improve. The average American household now has between $8,000 to $11,000 in consumer debt from credit cards alone! When you include student loans, car loans, home loans, medical bills, and loans from family members, you get the idea that the average American is awash in debt. Multiply this problem by the 300 million people in this country and it becomes apparent that this nation as a whole is in trouble. The fiscal distress extends to the federal government; the United States currently "enjoys" a federal budget deficit of more than $400 billion per year and a cumulative debt load of over $7 trillion! I don't want my community (that is you) to follow the path to financial slavery that has been chosen by the rest of the country.

Once you have made the decision to break out of financial chaos, commit to a system (any system), and then implement it. This book describes one good system. Good because it works, and even more so because it is simple. During the writing of this book, a population of people volunteered to be mentored by me in this process of wealth accumulation, and I will be reporting on their progress throughout the coming chapters. I will be telling you some of the stories that moved people from financial failure to success – and a few sad tales of the reverse. Yes, there are those who deviated from the conserver lifestyle and chose to remain in debt, or even to dig deeper.

I gave a two-day financial independence seminar in November of 2004. It is from this seminar that the mentoring population was derived. It started with 113 people who requested my services as a financial mentor. As I discuss the philosophy of wealth accumulation and the universal principles required to succeed, I will be sharing with you the stories of families, single adults and students from this population. The group was diverse in its phases of life. There were youths who had just arrived at college, had no job, and were getting help from family members.

There were single people who had just graduated from college and were looking for ways to control their expenses and save money. There were newly weds and young families with a new house payment and one or more car payments to pay down. And there were established families with up to 13 children who were looking for ways to save for retirement and yet not take food away from the table. Their stories have been included with the hope of inspiring you to make the choice to follow this simple path to financial success and a more fulfilled, more prosperous, and much calmer life.

Through the process of mentoring these participants, I discovered to my surprise that many people have emotional barriers to becoming wealthy. I found myself frequently advising them to give themselves permission to become wealthy. Many had the viewpoint that to be truly great Christians they had to live in poverty as the prophets of old did. I was a bit flummoxed by this concept originally, but encouraged them to see themselves as children of the Universe who, in order to carry out their purpose, had to fulfill the need for money in their lives. Once money was seen as a neutral tool to be wielded to achieve both daily objectives and truly grand purposes, the emotional barriers to accumulating wealth seemed to dissolve. Saving money became not a proof of miserly selfishness on their part but rather a means of providing more complete and timely service to others.

You, too, can harness the power of money for your own goals. Just remember the basic five principles for wealth accumulation:

Create Your Financial Goals – vision

Live Within Your Means – *if* you haven't got it, don't spend it

Pay Yourself First – save for those emergencies

Pay It Forward – save for your retirement

Philanthropy – take care of your community

Do you want financial freedom? It can be yours, starting today. Just choose, and implement the principles of financial freedom outlined in the following pages. You will be amazed by the increase in wealth and contentment in your life.

Chapter 2:

Creating Your Financial Plan

You may have had prior training in goal setting and creating time lines for various business or community projects. Why not start applying that training to your finances as well?

Find Your Purpose

The first step in the process of wealth accumulation is defining your life's purpose. I find this is the most challenging step in all of goal setting. If you have no idea why you are here on planet Earth, then you will continue to flounder and coast through life without focus or direction. The absence of focus is what has led you to your current fiscal situation. Are you happy with it? Has it benefited you? You must begin now to create a direction, one which will guide you not only today, but tomorrow and next year and in two decades. What you need is Vision.

I start my financial mentoring sessions by asking my clients the question, "Okay, what is your purpose in life?" I usually get a blank look or a quick answer like, "To be a good mother," or "To provide for my family," or (if they choose to be really honest) "I have no idea, Janine."

One of the tools that helps break down the quick answers and unlocks what you truly want out of life is to *write your own obituary*. Most people find this a bit shocking at first, but once they sit down to write, the ideas start flowing. What is it that you want people to say about you when you are gone? What type of person were you? What type of life did you live? Were you a philanthropist? Did you serve on county commissions? Were you a stay-at-home mom who ran a successful business from her garage? Were you a corporate professional that dropped the $100,000 a year job to follow your passion for car repair? You get the idea.

When you think about writing your obituary, most of the objections that you have to doing grand things now dissolve because you are writing in the past tense. This is an incredibly powerful technique. You write a description of your life as it happened (at least in your dreams), and you don't worry about whether or not you had enough money or your family disagreed with your life choices or that your spouse would never, ever agree to live off-grid in Colorado. Just write the story of your life as if it had already occurred and you will allow yourself to see your real passions in life and what values and activities you truly hold dear.

Occasionally, a person will have difficulty writing their obituary because of the morbid nature of the document, so I tell them, "Hey, what would your best friend say after you're gone?" Then, they knuckle down and start writing the eulogy speech that they want their best friend to give at the funeral. What matters here is not the name of the document, but the intent of this piece.

Create Your Legacy

I want you to decide what the outcome of your entire life's efforts will be. How do you want to be remembered? What do you want to build? What do you want to do? What experiences do you want to have before you leave this plane of existence? After your obituary is written, you then see clearly what is important to you. Is it to start your own business? Do you want to have a degree in medicine? Are you excited about becoming a basketball pro? Whatever the accomplishments you wish to have achieved, *now* is the time to start making your dreams, your Vision, into a catalog of worthwhile accomplishments.

Having written your life's story in advance, you rework the data from the obituary into a purpose statement. A good way to start is by examining good ideas from other people. Some examples from a few successful individuals include:

Walt Disney: "To make people happy."

Henry Ford: "To mass produce, mass distribute, and have cars mass consumed."

Andrew Carnegie: "To manufacture and market steel."

Mother Teresa: "To care for and comfort the poor, sick and needy all over the world."

My personal two-fold purposes in life are: "To demonstrate the principles of wealth accumulation through debt-free living," and "To teach others to be conservers rather than consumers." My family's purpose statement is to "Be as simple as you can be to reveal the beauty within."

Write It Down

Once you know what your purpose is, write it down. This is the step in goal setting that so many people try to skip.

When you know what you want, *write it down*. The simple act of taking a thought, idea or dream and putting it on paper brings the concept out of your head and manifests it strongly in our three-dimensional world. It is not enough to think about your purpose. Thoughts have little power to shape our daily existence unless they have been brought into this plane of existence. The power of "self-fulfilling prophecy" is in this process. You truly can create your own future if you take the responsibility to write down what it is you want to do in this life.

By committing your thoughts to paper, you signal your unconscious mind to start working on the challenges that are currently in your way. Your vision becomes so clear and strong in your mind that immediately your behaviors and opportunities will be changed as you move toward this new idea. While working on your purpose statement, don't worry with how you're going to achieve anything. Just figure out what you want to do. You are working on the *why* part of your life right now, not the *how*. The *how* is worked out later.

Who Will You Be in Years to Come?

Now that you have your purpose statement and obituary, it is time to start setting goals.

Start with 20-year goals. What kind of person do you want to be in 20 years? What will you have created? What will you have accomplished? What are some of the behaviors or degrees or skills that you will have acquired in 20 years? Write them down. Then we cut the time in half and write out 10-year goals. Write out goals for 5 years, then again for 2.5 years, and then focus hard on the next 12 months.

Be methodical on this one. Take your time writing out what you are going to do over the next 12 months to achieve the previously stated long-term goals. As one of my mentors, Dr. Oliver DeMille, is fond of saying, "People usually underestimate what they can do in 20 years and overestimate what they can do in a single year." You really want to make sure that you do not over-commit yourself on this first year.

The mere fact that you are taking the time to write out your goals puts you in the elite of America. Studies have shown that only 3 % of us actually have written goals, and of that 3% only 2% rewrite and refer to them on a regular basis. This is the power of forward thinking. I don't think it is coincidence that the truly wealthy of our country (those with incomes or wealth over $1.1 million) also make up the top 3% of the U.S. population. Coincidence? I think not!

Why is writing your goals so important? One study in the 1950s of Yale graduates says it all. Each graduate was asked if they had goals for their future. Only 3% of these students had written goals. Years later, when the follow-up survey was given, it was found that the 3% with written goals not only achieved them, but that their net worth was as much as the other 97% of their classmates combined. Don't skip over this step of goal setting! It is a way for you to implant firmly in your mind the need for behavior modification if you wish to accomplish all the wonderful things you set down in your obituary. You may have heard this study quoted before, but I still say, "Wow!" every time I read it. This is the power of the written goal. It is unfortunate so few of us use them. We are more productive and make better decisions with written goals then most of us can without them. Whenever a decision needs to be made, you can keep your focus by asking, "Is this new responsibility, job, or opportunity in line with my purpose?" Very quickly your life takes on new meaning and you find you have more energy to accomplish what you want to do. Decide now to be among that 3% of America that actually writes down goals so that you can achieve what you want out of life.

Now this sounds like a lot of work. But I have timed myself and I have timed my clients. Some of them have told me, "Janine, I'm not going to do this unless you're sitting across the table from me." I say, "Okay, but can I iron my shirts while you work?" I end up agreeing to mother hen them if that is what they need from me. Sometimes people just want to be babysat while they are writing goals. The longest it has taken was 45 minutes. This is not time-consuming because once you have your purpose statement and once you've written down what a wonderful person you were on the planet, the goal setting just happens. My husband and I can whip this stuff out in 15 to 20 minutes. And we do it on a regular basis, so that we can continually rework our goals to more effectively serve our individual and common purposes.

But What About the Money?

One of the most frequent responses I get after this exercise is, "But Janine, none of my goals have a thing to do with money!" That is when I get to chuckle and say, "Of course!"

Please remember that money is a tool. It is like a hammer. Money is the means to reaching your goals, and should not be the goal itself. Money is neither evil nor good. How you choose to use it determines the outcome. In order to build something in this life you need the appropriate tools to accomplish it. If you want to build a bird house, you're going to require the use of a saw, hammer, boards, nails, wire, a bit of glue (and a bird!). In order to build an organization, create a business, or start a foundation, you will need the tool of money. Naturally, your goals will not reflect monetary amounts unless those monetary amounts drive the creation of your dreams. It is best not to focus on specific dollar amounts so that you don't unnecessarily create a barrier to your success – or limit the extent to which the Universe showers you with fiscal blessings. If you adopt limits in your fiscal life, you will achieve them. No more, and no less.

Take Action

The goals that you set will require action. You don't want these daily or monthly action items to cause you stress. You can eliminate the stress of the action items by making sure that what you want (your purpose) is really what *you* want. Not your parents, not your spouse, not the rest of the community, but *you*. Then there is joy in doing the activities that are moving you toward your annual goals. The motivation will be self-materializing as long as the goals you have set were of your own creation, and reflect your own deepest desire.

Ask yourself some questions to assist in determining what you want from this life. What makes me truly happy? When am I the happiest? For some people it is, "When I'm with a person I care about and we've just climbed to the top of a mountain," or "When I'm running on the beach," or "When I'm spending more time playing with my kids." I had one gentleman whose purpose was to feed and clothe the poor as well as raise a solid family. He told me he didn't know how to integrate the two. I told him, "Well, take your family with you." And the light bulb went on and he said, "Oh, right." I continued, "You don't have to do this alone! See how many other people you can take with you on your purposeful life. Build an organization to do this." And he has. He routinely travels on business with his family, and he has built a very efficient business. In short, he is very successful both professionally (as assessed in monetary terms) and personally (as defined by contentment). Clearly, money isn't the only measure, or even the most important measure, of being rich.

So what are your values, and what do you stand for or believe in? What are you willing to die for? Commit right now to live and spend your life in fulfillment of your core values. This will tell you whether or not these values are yours or only values you (or others) "think" you should have. Are you willing to commit right now to it? Write yourself a contract. This worked for one of my clients; he was an attorney. He sat down, worked up a contract, signed and dated it. It was going to take him seven years to achieve his goals, and he did it in three just by writing a contract to himself. This is the power of writing your thoughts down.

Every Three Months

It seems to me but a small sacrifice to deny myself sleep so that I can stay up and rewrite my goals. Oh, didn't I tell you? You rewrite your goals every 3 months. Yes, that is correct: *every three months.*

Come on, now, stop rolling your eyes and moaning. Your life is not static! You need to constantly update your goals. By doing this you can tell if you are getting off track or if you are staying in line with your purpose. Just this month I had my late night appointment with myself to rework my goals. I laughed at how much my business plan had changed. I had decided to drop one business model for another simply because it was not in line with my purpose. Had I not rewritten my goals, I would not have received the "pat on the back" that I got from this change. Don't discount those moments of inner triumph we get from accomplishment – even seemingly minor ones. Those moments when you get a surge of adrenalin and think to yourself, "Yeah, I'm on track." "I'm doing what needs to be done!" "That was the right choice." These moments keep you energized and happy. They make the journey of purpose worthwhile. They keep you motivated.

Your Needs are Finite

Before you start your goal setting, please realize a few basic truths. The first fundamental truth is that our real needs are finite. Our basic needs are easily obtained. What is it that we truly require of life? We need food, clothing and shelter, and in some cultures maybe a car. It is our wants that are infinite, and not our needs. Just ask any three-year-old! They will tell you that they want everything!

Once you realize that you can't have everything that you want, you're golden! For some reason, many of us (even after decades in the school of life) are still living the lie that we can have it all. We believe that being rich means inexhaustible resources. Joe Dominguez mentions this in *Your Money or Your Life*: "When you are financially independent, the way money functions in your life is determined by you and not by your circumstances." That is a powerful statement when you're starting to do your goals. You then understand that the reason money has been such an obstacle in your past has been due to your choices. Once you have your plan written down, your brain will then start saying, "How do I get more cash?" and "What do I do with it when I get it?" and "What can I do for somebody to serve them so that this enterprise will make more money?" The emphasis is on money, yes, but it is on money in service of your Vision. And such noble dreams have a way of mobilizing the Universe to send more and more opportunities for money into our lives.

What Do *You* Want?

The next truth to understand is to *know what you really want* and not what you think you want because of societal pressures.

Learn to know when you have had enough. For anyone who has ever been on a diet, that is a big challenge. Mainly, because when we're talking about our food, everything tastes so wonderful. To learn to know when you've had enough takes training. It is going to take you some time, but you will begin to see it. I had a client who learned of a neighborhood family that would share a single coat among their five children. She asked her neighbor boy where his coat was since he was shivering at the school bus stop. He answered her, "It is my cousin's turn to wear the coat." She then learned of the family's hardship. My client's first reaction to learning about this situation was to run home and start unloading her closets of extra coats. She was able to come up with five coats for this family. She passionately said to me, "I am going to take care of those kids!" If you react responsibly to what you already own, then you'll open up space for other things to come into your life. So, learn when you've had enough and stop making unnecessary purchases.

We are weird as a culture when it comes to making plans. We create five-year plans and only update them once a year! On January 1st we set up New Year's Resolutions, and then we don't revisit them until January of the next year. I can tell you that in the last three months I have reworked my short-term goals five times. I received new information, I obtained different resources, I found a different vision, whatever you want to call it. So these goals are not in stone. How can they be? If the target shifts, the goals have to change as well. That is why I don't want you to spend hours on them. But at least, have some idea of where you're going because your purpose statement is going to drive how you make the changes in your goals. At the end of three months I can ask you, "How are your goals looking?" You're going to laugh at me and you'll have to say, "I had to scrap them and start over." Exactly. That is a good thing.

Don't make a goal and think you are a quitter if you don't stick to it. Too much is going to change in your life. Maybe you have taken on a few too many activities and you need to back off and regroup. Maybe the system you chose to implement these goals is faulty and by changing the system you realized you needed to change the goals, too. You may have created a goal and found that you're trying to accomplish the wrong item at the wrong phase of your life. Failure is not a negative. It is actually an opportunity to change your present, and in doing so to select the best possible future. It is how the Universe redirects you so that you can *really* accomplish something bigger then you think yourself capable. How can you grow the mental, financial and spiritual muscles to create your vision if you don't have a few challenging events occur that require you to fall back and regroup before surging forward again? Possibly you will move just enough to one side that you rocket ahead to your vision of what you are to do in life. Accept a failure, as these happen to all of us. But never accept a failure as a final defeat. Failure is only an opportunity to redirect our efforts along a new and different path. This is a definition of success. Given persistence and enough time, the knowledge gained by failures plants the seeds for success – in life, and in financial independence.

Two Common Questions on Goals:

1. *These goals, are they couple goals or individual goals?*

Yes! Both! Are you identical to your spouse? As an individual you have something to contribute to this Universe, and then as a dyad you have something else to offer. Each set of goals are going to be unique. You're going to have different strengths. What my husband and I do is we work on our goals individually for 15 to 20 minutes. Then we come back and look at our goals; they are almost always in line. What do we do if they aren't in line with one another (because Janine has come up with another of her bizarre ideas)? We just take some time to discuss it, to figure out if it is in line with our combined purpose at all, and whether the time to implement it is going to be now or later. Simple, huh? It just takes practice.

2. Is there a contradiction between a "now" and a "future" goal?

Only to a linear thought process. I was raised in Japan and so I have a very warped viewpoint on this (as my husband will tell you). It was hard for me to get used to the American way of thought. There is no contradiction for me in what I am doing day by day and the goals I have aiming for 100 years down the road. Yes, I have goals 100 years away. I want my legacy to impact future generations. I know what I do today is going to affect at least three generations. If you believe certain types of Hindu philosophy, up to seven generations will be affected. Don't be afraid of making those long-term goals and thinking you can't handle it.

Let's Try Early Retirement!

At this point in the wealth accumulation process you are now armed with three very important pieces of information.   You have your obituary, your purpose statement, and your goals for the next 20 years. You now have a level of focus that you probably haven't had before. *Now* is the time that you sit down and say, "Okay, how in the world am I going to pay for it all?" What are your financial goals? This is the time of reckoning. How much debt do you have? How are you going to pay it off? What is the plan you're going to use to pay it off? You might say, "Well, it would be helpful to have our own home so that we can stop renting." So, you start saving for a house. Or maybe you want to go to college. You may want to retire before age 65! I focus on early retirement because this is where my husband, Brad, totally thought his wife had lost her mind!

He comes home from work one day about ten years ago and I pounce on him with a cheery "Honey, I've got a plan! You're going to retire by 50!" (Brad was 36 years old at the time.) He just stares at me and says, "Okay, it has been a long week and I know you've been home alone with the six-month-old, but what are you blithering about?" This is the point when I had learned enough of the fundamental principles of financial success from all my reading and practicing that I was able to come up with a plan. I knew that to achieve our combined purpose (a simple healthy childhood for our son, and the ability for us to improve our community by teaching and writing) Brad had to be able to retire from his job. Working at a full-time corporate position for another 25 years was contradictory to our long-term purpose as a family. I had been working on this plan all day. I was excited after struggling with it, trying to come up with a way to achieve this goal. I had finished reading Amy Dacyczyn and Joe Dominguez. I said to my husband that I had figured it all out, and in 14 years we would become financially independent and not need to work at all. My reception to this spectacular news was answered with dead silence and looks of pity. So I explained that if I really cut our expenses and we invested the savings that this scheme would work. I showed him all of my charts and the plan and how we were going to do it. His reaction was, "Honey, it will never work, but go ahead!" That is what I love about my husband; most people would think me an absolute cracked personality, but he supported me anyway. Instead of 14 years, we became financially independent in seven years using my initial plan, with periodic readjustments along the way. That whole journey was incredible, and the day we became financially independent was even more fantastic. Along the way we had so many wonderful opportunities and resources showered upon us that we felt bludgeoned over the head. And you know what? We still do, and we can't shovel those monetary and material gifts out the door fast enough. After all, we're only conduits, not the end users of this largesse. If you want to retire before the age of 65, it is possible once you establish a plan, because the Universe helps you along once It knows that you are serious.

Be Specific

That is why writing your goals down is so important. Whatever financial goals you have, start writing them down. I will ask my clients, "What are your financial goals?" and they tell me, "I want to be filthy rich." I say, "Okay, what does that look like?" I mean, I don't mind you being filthy rich, but what does that look like to you? You have to set a specific financial amount. For anyone who is in debt, you have an exact financial amount, don't you? You know what you owe every month when the statement comes in. You can't get more exact then that, can you? You know exactly what you need to get out of debt.

For my husband's peace of mind, he told me he wouldn't feel financially secure until we had more money in our short-term savings account. I asked him, "Honey, how much is that? How much will you need to feel secure?" Give me an exact number. He selected a figure equal to six months of expenses, the amount of time he figured it would take to get his consulting business started. (He got his first client three weeks after leaving corporate America for the self-employed life.) So for those of you who are out of debt and you want to know what sort of a nest egg to have in a money market fund, one idea is to figure out your monthly expenses and your annual insurance premiums and the deductibles on all your insurance policies and pretend that you would be required to cough up that cash for the whole year all at once. That is a good starting point. Many of the books and articles I have read on money management suggest that you have three to six months of expenses. You'll work up to that, but for starters and for a shorter goal, try working up to a figure of all your insurance deductibles. Then work up to three, six, and twelve months worth of salary. Set exact financial amounts in your financial goals. This brings power to your vision.

Make Your Dream Three-Dimensional

Once you set your financial amounts down, create a picture or image of your dream, whatever it is. Owning your own home, starting your own business, going to college, travel. Then draw a picture, cut out a picture, make a collage, or use clay to make a model. Create a detailed three-dimensional image of your vision. When you write your plans down on paper that is one way of getting your goals into our four-dimensional world, but working up a model or pictorial representation is an even more powerful way of creating a concrete vision for your future. You will look at this image every day. For families I suggest that you put the picture on the refrigerator and tape it at eye level for most of the kids. The next time they are begggging you for a Chocolate Frosted Sugar Cereal, you can tell them, "We can have the brand name sugary cereal, or you can go with the generic so that we will be X dollars closer to our dream." Then point emphatically to the family's visional picture. (Pasting a look of triumph on your face is also permissible.) That is how you get your family involved too; even little children who can't read will come to understand the image. For those of you who are single, I say put your dream in a conspicuous place and build a little community of friends who are doing the same thing. That way you can have a support system to say, "Guess what? I paid off X number of credit cards! Yeah!" Throw a party (using cheaper generic brands, of course) and pat yourself on the back.

The Wise Man and the Teenage Entrepreneur

When I was 15 years old, I had the exceptionally good fortune of chatting with the late Sam Walton, the co-founder of Wal-Mart. When I met him, I didn't know who he was. My father was kind enough not to tell me Mr. Walton's name until after we were heading for home, as my behavior to him was more than a bit conceited – not that one is shocked when an arrogant teenager (like there is really any other kind) is a bit full of herself....

Nevertheless, I felt that my conceit / confidence in this situation was well-founded, for Mr. Walton and I met during the course of my business. As I look back on it, Mr. Walton and I shared a fascinating conversation. The old gentleman (which was how I thought of him at the time, of course) asked me what I was doing, and I said that I was an entrepreneur (I was cleaning a client's house at the time, and he had come in for a glass of water.)

He smiled at me and said, "Oh really? Good for you. By the way, I like those shoes you have on."

I replied, "Thanks. I paid $60 for them, which took me four months, but they're worth it because my feet don't hurt."

He said, "Those aren't from Wal-Mart, are they?"

I said, "Oh no! No one with sense buys ladies shoes at Wal-mart! They stink. They're awful."

He responded, "Really? Why is that?"

"Well, they fall apart. They're not worth my money. And don't even think about clothes! I don't buy them because they fade and fall apart after two to three washes. I have to buy men's wear to get my money's worth at Wal-Mart!"

"The old gentleman" was incredible. He taught me so much about value and running a business in five minutes. You know what he said to me?

"So you have to walk around looking androgynous because you can't find quality women's clothing that you can afford?"

I replied, "Exactly. I have to pay too much money. And the reason I started this business is to buy a car, not clothes." I said this while scrubbing out the client's kitchen sink.

He said, "I know the manager at your local Wal-Mart. If I were to assure you that the women's clothing would be better in a few months, would you consider shopping at Wal-Mart again?"

I was amused. "Well, what are you, the *owner* or something?"

He smiled. "I know him very well."

"If you're in with the owner, fine. I'll give it another try."

He said, "Give it 30 days."

Mr. Walton put his glass on the counter and walked outside. I was in the process of putting my cleaning supplies into my bike basket when he walked over to me for a final word and said, "Since you're an entrepreneur, would you like some simple advice?"

I responded, "Yes, I would, because I'm not going to do this forever. This is not who I am, but I'm doing it now to get where I want to go."

He ticked off points on his fingers. "Number one, the customer is always right. And number two, learn to replicate yourself." Those were his two pieces of advice to me. And Sam Walton did just that with Wal-Mart. He trained people to have the same love and caring for customers whether they were in upper management or a stock clerk in the health and beauty department. So that philosophy filtered down. True to his word, in 30 days the quality of product went way up in the local Wal-Mart, and women started buying clothes there again as word spread.

More importantly, his words of advice live on today. Think about it. When you walk into almost any Wal-Mart and ask an associate where something is, they will get down off that ladder and show you. Where does that attitude come from? That comes from upper management. You may not be running your own business as you read this, but I still want you to take Mr. Walton's advice and learn to replicate yourself. By duplicating yourself and your purposeful life, you achieve greater impact in your community. When you're purpose is strong enough, it will inspire other people and *they will help you in achieving what you want* out of life. I see it all the time in people that I mentor. They get a passion. They see the light at the end of the tunnel, and they see that their $15,000 debt is going to be gone in three more years, and they are already thinking about what they are going to do next to move them toward their purpose.

I have since read that Sam Walton would sit down once a week with his staff to set the goals for the coming week. This meeting was not allowed to last for longer than ten minutes. Walt Disney did the same thing in building the Magic Kingdom. He met every morning and evening with his immediate staff for <u>ten minutes</u> to go over the day's events. Both men and the organizations they led were constantly reevaluating their goals so that they did not loose track of their purpose. One of Walt Disney's most quoted sayings when it comes to his business ventures was, "Please remember that this all started with a Mouse." <u>He didn't want people to get too serious about work.</u>

Time to Start Talking to Yourself

Now, you've written your purpose. You've written your goals. You know what you want to accomplish this year. The next step is to work your annual goals into affirmations.

That's right, GOAL affirmations. There is plenty of literature out there by leading psychologists who will tell you all about why and how affirmations achieve their effectiveness. Do they work? Of course they do (or I wouldn't be telling you about them). Not only do I know from personal experience that they work, but I know from business associates the power that these little beauties possess.

There are some simple rules that you should follow when creating your affirmations. First, know that what you are trying to do is to program your subconscious mind with the main thoughts from your conscious mind. You must be careful in your statements so as not to "feed" your subconscious mind thoughts it frankly won't believe. So, in your statements be sure to make them present tense. They must state things in the here and now. Second, say them out loud. Don't fight me here!!! I know what I'm talking about! Go hide in a closet, the bathroom, or sit alone in the car and say them out loud as you drive to work. You'll think yourself silly, crazy, or just plain stupid, but it *works*. This is only the beginning of the many psychological tricks I am going to suggest to help you out of your current financial difficulties. So, get used to it!

Write down a single affirmation that will assist you in your self-esteem or self-confidence so that you can achieve your goals, and then say it out loud every day. The more you say it, the more likely it will be to manifest in your life. By saying affirmations out loud you're telling the Universe, "I want *this*. And I want it in *this* time frame." The Universe knows that I'm one determined individual and that I don't take "no" for an answer. (Talk to my friends! My husband, Brad, will be only too happy to tell you how stubborn I am.) I have a very strong will, but I use it to good effect to gain what I want in this life by regularly employing the power of positive affirmations.

After you say them out loud, then make your plan to achieve them. This is where planning is important. Now is the time to create a plan, not before. Don't try to figure out a plan when you're working on your purpose. You can't implement a plan if you don't know what you are planning for. I'm going to say this again because it is really important. *Planning does not achieve purpose.* You must have vision first. Got it? Good.

I used to have many thoughts that would try to beat me up as I learned the tools of wealth accumulation. Stupid worries would creep into my brain, trying to keep me down. "Too bad you made that purchase before you read *Your Money or Your Life.* Look at all the money you could have saved if you had known these principles back then. Imagine what you could have done with all that cash you wasted." You get the idea. These thoughts were constantly haunting me as I strove to learn how to be a conserver. I used affirmations to stop them from continually looping through my brain. The one that worked for me was, "Yes, but I am a different person now." This simple statement applied to the negative self-talk has completely defeated my internal adversaries. Don't hesitate to use affirmations. They really do work. Even if your husband looks up from his paper and says, "Were you talking to me, babe?"

Chapter 3:

The 60 / 40 Principle

You now have four documents: your obituary, your purpose statement, your goals, and your affirmations. With these in tow, it is time to move on to the next phase.

Live Within Your Means

I heard this advice so much while I was learning to be a conserver. Every time someone would say it to me or that I would read this trite piece of advice, my first reaction was, "Right, but HOW!?" I felt like screaming at the top of my lungs, I heard and read it so much. Everyone said it, but no one could show me how.

Maybe you were lucky and learned how from your parents. But that's not likely, or you would not be reading my book! I certainly did not learn how in my family. My family's money model growing up was not conducive to wealth accumulation. My friends and associates were no better off than Brad and I were at the time, so I didn't want to go down the same path that they did. Unfortunately, I couldn't find a model that taught me how to manage my finances responsibly. I didn't know the basic principles of husbanding money. Now I do. Let me share them with you.

Money Flows

Simply put, money is not static. If you accept this one universal principle, that money flows, you are on your way to understanding wealth accumulation.

There are three firmly entwined arms that comprise the cycle of money. These three elements keep money moving through the Universe. If at any time all three are not being implemented, you'll see a break in the flow of money into and through your life. A feeling of deprivation will set in, and you'll be reaching for credit cards to fill the gap.

The three arms that determine the flow of money are Living, Saving, and Giving (Figure 1):

Figure 1:   The Flow of Money

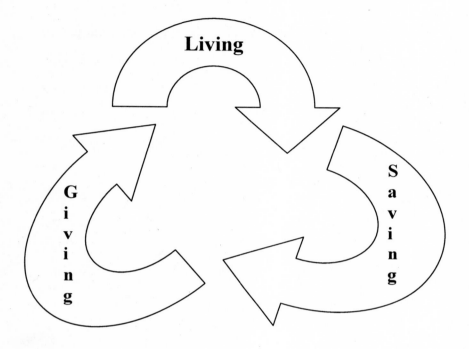

Believe it or not, we are not supposed to live on 100% of our take-home income. We need to drastically readjust our thinking and realize that we are to live on only (drum roll here, please) 60% of our income! That's right, only 60% of your income is yours to spend on stuff! The Universe will handle everything in your financial life to your great satisfaction if you learn to live consistently on only 60% of your income. I can hear you now. "But Janine, I have $15,000 in credit card debt, a house payment, car payments and medical bills, and you're telling me I only have 60% of my hard-earned money to use for my own wants and needs. Are you nuts? How on earth do I get to that level considering my debt load?" Good questions all. And I will get to them. First, though, hear me out on where the other 40% goes. I will be giving you some systems on how to implement this whole process.

This is the way that the 60 / 40 rule breaks down your income. If you're only supposed to be Living on 60% of your income, where does the rest of it go? Here you are:

Figure 2:   The Division of Money

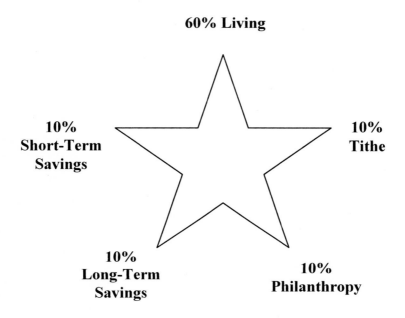

60% Living

10% Short-Term Savings

10% Tithe

10% Long-Term Savings

10% Philanthropy

From Figure 2 you can see that the remaining 40% of your income is divided up into the other two arms of money, the Saving and Giving elements of the cycle (each of which gets 20% of your take-home pay).

Let's start with Savings, the part where you *pay yourself first!* That's right, the very first thing you do with your money, if you really want to accumulate wealth, is to pay yourself 20% of your take-home pay. Why? Because if you don't keep it now, you'll never get it back. You will have lost both the money you earned in the first place, and the entire opportunity for your savings to grow and bring you even more money. So resolve now to start treating yourself as the most important debt that you owe. *Saving something for yourself is the major fundamental principle of financial freedom.*

And here's how to do it right. The first 10% of Savings goes into Long-Term Savings. For most of us this is our retirement fund, money that we should NEVER spend until we reach 65 years of age (if then)! The next 10% of Savings goes into Short-Term Savings. This is money that you use to pay for expenses you know are coming your way, such as car insurance, property taxes, maintaining your car, and new appliances. This is also the savings account you use when the unexpected happens.

You use the money in this account to pay for emergencies rather than reaching for your credit card. Why? Because you don't want to dig your way deeper into debt and bury your chances for financial independence by not being able to pay for relatively small expenditures.

Having paid yourself, now it's time to give back, to take care of others. Not your family; their needs comes from the Living arm of the money cycle. The 20% of your money dedicated to this Giving goes to the community, to worthy projects that will improve the world around you. This dispersal of money represents Giving in the truest sense. And the Universe will acknowledge the debt It owes you by sending more money your way – as long as you Give.

The first form of Giving is the 10% of your income that you dedicate as a Tithe. I want you to see this money as rent. It is the rent you pay the Universe for being a human being on the planet Earth. You walk across the ground of this planet, eat the food grown upon it, breathe the air, and enjoy the beauty that surrounds us. This 10% is the rent you pay for the mere privilege of being alive. If you do not have a religious affiliation, then give this tithe money to a group or institution that you feel is doing good works for humanity. The other 10% of the Giving arm is allocated to Philanthropy. Yes, this is money that you just give away because other people have needs that exceed your own. This money needs to go to an organization of your choice that is doing good deeds in line with your particular passions and purpose statement. Not family in the immediate sense, but family in the true community sense. Later on, in the discussion on Philanthropy (Chapter 7), I will explain how you make sure that your charitable money is being used well.

Now let's take some time to examine more closely the 40% of your income that does not get directed to your daily wants and needs. We'll start with savings. Why? Because savings is where you pay yourself first, the point at which you actually take some of your money and set it aside to help you accumulate wealth to benefit you. Sounds good, right? It is.

Saving for Your Golden Years

Your Long-Term Savings account goes by several other names depending on who you talk to. This is your nest egg that is in the form of specialized retirement investments (401k, 403b, and IRA [individual retirement account] vehicles). This money is going to take care of you and your spouse when you can no longer work for income or when you choose to no longer work.

You never touch this money while you're under the age of 65! I don't care if your father needs heart surgery. I'm not kidding. Why? Because a true principle of conscious living is to look out for Number One first – and that Number One is you. Not your parents, not your children, but you and you alone. (And your spouse, of course, because the "you " here is the team that has the combined sense of purpose that drives your family's Vision.) This focus is not selfish, as some would have you believe, but in fact demonstrates quite clearly that you understand the real virtue of self-reliance. That long-term savings account is your safety net, the one that you will depend on because no one else is going to take care of you – not your family or the government. It's up to you.

You need to fund a long-term savings account, and fund it well and early, to take full advantage of compound interest. It is the lack of understanding about compound interest that has many people trapped in the dodgy financial position that they find themselves in today. People think that they can give themselves a loan on their 401k and can simply "pay themselves back" at a later time. Money does not grow that way. You're effectively robbing yourself of principal and earning potential that could have been worth as much as three times the amount that you pulled from the account. Place this money in your retirement plan and *leave it there*! Don't think of it again until you need it in retirement. Now, if you don't have a 401k plan, or the plan you do have will not allow you to save 10% of your income, then put the remainder of the 10% into a savings account at your local bank until it becomes $1500 to $2500; then move it into an individual investment vehicle of some kind, like a traditional IRA or Roth IRA.

Why are long-term investments so important? Because when you get old and grey and can't do for yourself anymore, that money is going to pay you like a paycheck does now. We all know that social security is going to be there for us, right? (Yes, this is sarcasm.) "The government has got me taken care of! I'm going to get a couple of hundred bucks a month from them and I'm going to be able to live on it!" That is how many Americans live right now. They don't want to think about their long-term financial future because they see no way to save money when they are burdened by incredible amounts of consumer debt. Maybe they couldn't save enough for a truly rich retirement. But even a little bit salted away now will provide for a much better future than they will "enjoy" if they make no effort at all to act on their own behalf.

Keeping Credit Cards at Bay

Your Short-Term Savings account is the savings account that you spend when the tires need to be replaced, a child needs braces, the property taxes are due. For these regular but intermittent expenditures, you pull the money from here. Not, repeat *not*, from credit cards. Your short-term savings account is to deal with known expenses as well as the ones that pop up unexpectedly. We all know these expenses: the furnace breaks down in the dead of winter, a water heater leaks all over the basement, or your washing machine finally dies and the repairman tells you it will cost more to fix it than to replace it.

Most people have only one savings account and they call it their "rainy day fund." However, they forget to define in their mind exactly "what is a rainy day?" The rainy day for them is every day, because expenses are always popping up in their lives; they find themselves constantly pulling money from the account and are unable to put any back. Part of your one-year goals is to sit down and figure out what your expenses are going to be for the following year. How much do I need to save for car registration, insurance premiums, house repair, and medical deductibles? And that is when your spouse says, "Have you seen the car's tires? Aren't they supposed to have at least a little bit of tread?" Even though you don't have the money, start looking at tire sales now. When the money does arrive, you can best use it because you will already know what the true bargain prices will be. The thing here is preparation. The Boy Scout motto says it all: Be prepared. That is what this Short-Term account is for, the more than piddling daily expenses and the small emergencies that life is going to throw at us.

Now, of course, when you first sit down to do this, the primary thing that is going to happen is that the dishwasher is going to break and flood your kitchen and basement, requiring a fairly major reconstruction – and this may happen right after you put the new carpet down. These are the types of annoyances that are going to happen as you start down this path of wealth accumulation. The Universe is going to test you. Are you truly committed to doing this 60 / 40 principle or are you going to try to take the easy way out? Not that there is one, but everyone tries to find one. Let me know if you find it. I'm still looking, too.

Stay the Course Despite the Challenges

Remember the folks in my seminar who signed up for mentoring? More than 95% of them called me with a challenge to the 60 / 40 principle when they first started off using it. Because of this initial challenge, 34% of the people who requested mentoring dropped out of the study. They chose to go their own way rather than trust this proven system and stay with it. I don't know how well they did, because they stopped talking with me. The other 66% of my clients continued on with the full three months of financial coaching. The end result was that 95% of this latter group experienced an increase in their Long-term Savings accounts and 71% saw an increase in their Short-term Savings. I don't know about you, but such a large response after a relatively brief educational experience says it all. Any one can start to accumulate wealth, if they only know how. The students in my seminar learned, and now you know, too: 10% to Long-term savings, and 10% to Short-term savings, each and every time you get paid, without fail. Of course, the seminar students also chose to act on their new knowledge, a choice that you will have to make as well if you want to start building wealth. You will have to elect to Save.

So are you to the point where you hear yourself saying, "I'm tired of debt? I'm going to stop the debt, I'm going to stop the consumer cycle and I'm going to follow the 60 / 40 principle come what may." Once you really commit, work consciously to keep the Saving, Living, and Giving arms in balance, and don't break the cycle. Money will keep flowing in your life, and you will succeed.

Do Unto Others

Now that we've dealt with Saving for our own needs, let's move on to Giving for the benefit of others. Giving is where you freely offer a portion of your own hard-earned money to the Universe for the good of all. Why? Because such donations indicate your clear understanding of the true financial principle that by taking care of others you are actually taking care of yourself.

Again, we start by Giving 10% as a Tithe, merely as the rent we pay for being human beings on the planet Earth. By distributing this 10% to the flow of money, we are telling the Universe that we are willing to pay our fair share to support the community at large. (Don't worry about whether or not the other guy is paying his share; if he's not rich, he isn't!) If you do not have a church or are associated with one, then find an organization that you believe in and that is doing good work and give that 10% to them. The organization is not important. The only essential is to send the money on and let the Universe figure out how to use it for the common good.

The other 10% of Giving is directed to Philanthropy. Start giving money away to good causes. If you're in debt, your first reaction to this will be cold, hard fear. If you barely have enough money to make the minimum payments on your credit cards, how on earth are you supposed to be able to give money to support someone else? Let me start by saying, stay calm and breathe deeply. I'm getting to that part. When I was in college and I was making $6,000 a year, I was writing weekly philanthropic checks totaling $1.37. That was all I could afford. And I have people to this day tell me, "Why did you do that? It cost you 28 cents just to ship that through the mail!" (I'm dating myself here.) That isn't the point. We're trying to show the Universe that we're conscientious in our concern for others, and that we have faith in the Truth that "what goes around comes around." That we trust that money flows and that we are distributing our wealth in a responsible way, whatever the magnificent sum may be (some of you are laughing here, I know). Money is a major responsibility. I had one 15-year-old student of mine tell me, "Janine, there is just as much responsibility in saving money as there is in spending it!" Exactly. Money is power. And with anything that has power associated with it, there are choices that have to be made. Are you going to abuse the power you have or are you going to put it to good use for a grand purpose?

Two Common Questions on the 60 / 40 Principle:

1. Do you base the 60 / 40 division on your net income or your gross income?

This is a personal choice. My family and I use our net income to figure 60 / 40, because we never see the other monies that are "tithed" directly to the government. For employees of corporations, your net income is your take-home pay AND any pre-tax deductions you make to retirement accounts, purchase of saving bonds, or other elective purposes that go to benefit you. If you choose to use your gross income, go right ahead. The major issue in terms of keeping money moving through the cycle is that all three arms – Living, Saving, and Giving – are being filled at a consistent proportion from all your income sources.

2. How do you teach the 60 / 40 principle to kids?

For children it is a bit different, because they don't have quite the same living expenses as adults. (We hope!) Instead, the 60 / 40 rule for adults is flipped for them since they have major expenses coming up in their futures (a car, college tuition, starting a business) while their current needs are for the most part being met. Instead, teenagers and young adults should follow the 40 / 60 rule. If a young person has a job and has money flowing, I recommend to them that they use the 40% to live on and put 10% to tithe, 10% to philanthropy, 20% to long-term savings, and 20% to short-term savings. What is amazing is that most teenagers and young adults find that they don't *need* 40% to live on and actually will self-correct to attain an even higher savings rate. You want them to do this. You don't want to tell them how to spend or save their money. Let them make mistakes under your roof while they are young and the mistakes are easily correctable and have no permanent consequences. One young client of mine (age 12) was using the 40 / 60 rule and had saved $60 in his 40% "living" fund to buy a Bionicle Ice Village. (Don't ask.) This toy cost over $50. He asked me if it was a worthy expenditure, and I told him that he was the only one who could make that choice. It had taken him seven months of hard work to save that much money using the 40 / 60 rule. He eventually went ahead and bought it. Three weeks later he came back to me lamenting that the toy was definitely *not* worth the money he paid for it. I encouraged him by saying, "John, you'll never make that mistake again, will you?" He replied, "Nope, I sure won't. I worked too hard for that money to *blow* it like that." Aren't these the messages we want our kids to receive? "Make your own choices with your own money, and be prepared to enjoy the outcome (or, if necessary, suffer the consequences of your own poor choice). Use caution when spending money, be careful of what you buy, and make sure it is worth the time and effort it took you to earn the money!" Sure, all of us (including adults!) can learn from the past actions of others. However, the lessons that lead to wealth accumulation are definitely more telling and last longer when we make the mistakes with our own capital.

Chapter 4:

Live Within Your Means

The single best piece of financial advice after "Pay yourself first" is "**Don't spend more than you earn**." However, I firmly believe that the mere admonition to "live within your means" is not enough by itself. There must be an action item associated with this principle in order to make it a point that will work for you.

That action is to track every single expense.

Running the Family's Business

Yep, I see you now. You're rolling your eyes into the back of your head again. I'm serious here! It is time to stop running your family finances in a helter-skelter fashion. Starting today, I want you to realize that your family is a business. There isn't a successful business in the world that has sloppy books. If you want to make sure that you live within your means, then I strongly recommend that you start tracking where all that money is going.

Oh, and if you think your family finances are not a business, pause and look at how the marketing and advertising corporations get you to buy their products. *They* see *you* as *big business*. Really big! At least $3 billion dollars a year is spent by corporations in this country alone on advertising to get you to buy things. Think a moment: $3 billion dollars just in advertising and marketing. Wow! And what are you armed with to combat this onslaught? What information do you have at your immediate disposal to stop the temptations to purchase? To avoid the impulse buys? Those ever-present "Oh, it's only a $2 purchase" moments? Nothing, huh? Me either – except for my knowledge of the fundamental principles of financial independence. And the one that says "don't spend more than you earn" is the most powerful means of ignoring those incessant marketing messages.

This is about the point in most financial discussions where people start talking about budgets. I always ask them, "Why bother to budget, when you could be doing anything more worthwhile?" And that "anything" really means "everything." Any thing you want to do is more useful than time spent budgeting, because budgets just don't work. Let me tell you why.

When you budget, you lose control over your finances. Instead, your money is now controlling you. This is not how we wish to live. Most of us would like to think that we have control over our money. Budgets remove the control from us and make us feel like we're back in grade school. When you're good, you have money left over. When you're bad, you can't buy what you want because you already spent money in that category. You rebel and start justifying (in all sorts of inventive ways) why you need the latest beanie baby, shoes, or cordless drill. Budgets are like diets. Until you know what your psychological triggers are for spending money, you'll never begin to gain control over the emotions that dominate your financial life.

Accept and Deal with Your Emotions

That brings us to the major point in any financial plan. Emotions. Most of the books I've read on finances rarely mention the emotional side of money. It is this fact alone that causes most of us the majority of heartache from debts and overspending. We spend all our time on the "practical" aspects of money management, and we totally neglect the one side of ourselves that needs to be fed the most. If we were totally rational creatures, budgets would work. However, as much as you may like to think that your rational side runs it all, it doesn't. Male or female, adult or child, most of us "plan" our financial ventures by engaging the emotions rather than the math. Unhappiness and fear are the keys to our spending habits. These two emotions are used by marketers to get us to buy their products. You see it in almost all commercials. If you want love, buy this toothpaste. If you're afraid of blowing a job interview, use this deodorant. If you want more friends in your life, you need a second home in Aspen. Over and over again, every day of our lives, we are confronted by these images and sayings. How do you fight it?

Live Consciously

The answer is simple. Choose to live consciously. Just because you're physically awake does not mean you are living in real awareness. What are you doing and why? Why do you feel compelled to buy another cordless drill when you already have three? Is it really going to make building the dog house that much faster? What are you going to do with the time you save in building the dog house with the new drill? Will you spend more time with your family, or will you have to work longer to pay for all the new tools you bought?

Living consciously takes time and introspection. Most of us spend a great deal of time and money to sidestep thinking about why we are unhappy. Instead of avoiding the issues, it is time to take responsibility for them. After all, we're adults now (we hope, in body if not in spirit). It is our responsibility to look inside, even if it scares us, and to discover why we are behaving the way we are. When you neglect this practice, it gives rise to the symptoms we see today. We're working harder, spending more, and yet have less time to enjoy the things we love. Our garages (and even our rented storage units!) are cluttered with too much stuff. We have more clothes then we can wear, more food then we can eat, and more radios then we can hear – and yet we're still not satisfied.

What do we do? One of the first steps to living consciously is setting goals. You've done that. The next is to take control of your finances and stop avoiding the problems that may be lurking in the checkbook. If you have credit card debt, now is the time to open that wallet and pull out every single card out. (If you do not have credit card debt, I want to say first, "Congratulations!!" Second, please read this anyway. It is my hope that by reading this you can help someone in your life who is in debt.) Okay, you have all your credit cards on the table. Go to your desk or kitchen drawer where you store all the cards that are not in your wallet. Put them on the table with the others. I want you now, this very minute, to get out the scissors and start cutting every single card in half, but one. That's right, cut up every single card except one. Are you scared? Does this piece of advice cause you to have an adrenalin rush? Is your heart hammering at the mere thought of not having credit cards in your life? I'm sorry to tell you this, but you're addicted. You're addicted to plastic, and the "free" money that it represents. We hear about alcohol, nicotine, and caffeine addiction, but few people are discussing what financially plagues our nation. We have an addiction to money that is not ours, to borrowed coin. We are thieves. We are stealing and we don't even realize it. The saddest part of this is that we're stealing from ourselves and we think it is okay. We're stealing our peace of mind, happiness, and health every day that we charge a purchase that we can't afford.

Face the Plastic

Now, look at all those credit cards on your table again. The ones you have not yet shredded. I want you to then look around your house. Do you have enough? Do you have enough food in your cupboard? Do you have enough clothes to wear? Do you have a place you call home? Then stop waiting and cut up all of them except one. The lonely card that remains is to be put into a bowl of water and then placed into the freezer. After it is an ice cube, take it to your Mom, Dad, Brother, Aunt, Uncle or a friend you trust and let that bowl sit in *their* freezer. In case you ever need that card it will be there. For the time being, though, you don't want to have access to it. I used to tell my clients to cut up all their cards. The emotional block to doing this was so strong that I would have some break down crying, begging me not to make them do it. Or they would yell and tell me I had no right to ask such a thing. Or the worst response of all (for them): they would leave and never come back. And in doing so they were giving up their one best chance for financial freedom. The emotional tie to plastic is as real and compulsive as a heroin addict's need for drug. I've learned over the years to give people an out. To let you have a "chance" at debt through the remaining card. This seems to calm the fear to a manageable level.

Priming the Money Pump

Okay, you've cut up all the credit cards but one. You've put the lone survivor in a friend's freezer to prevent easy access. You can move on to the next phase of this process. This step is exactly the same as priming a pump or a small gas-powered engine. You use a small amount of money to start the larger flow of money from the Universe's storehouse into yours.

Do you have a penny jar? A place where you store all your loose change? Get these coins out and count them up. What you're going to do now is to initiate the flow of money into your life. Because of your past choices regarding money, you've blocked its flow. Right now you probably can't live on 60% of your take-home income. Am I right? So, what you're going to do is the next best thing. Continue to pay your bills as you have always done, but you're going to get some extra money moving in your life right now. I want you to implement the 60 / 40 principle this minute using the penny jar. Count out all your change and split it up. Put 60% into your checking account. Put 10% in a long-term savings account. If you don't have a retirement plan (either an IRA or a 401k at work), then open a second savings account at your bank and use it to start your "long-term savings." Next, 10% goes into your fluid (short-term) savings account to start building your emergency fund. Then, give 10% to a favorite charity, and the final 10% as a tithe to a church or charitable organization of your choice. By dividing your penny jar in this way, you're sending a signal to the Universe that you're serious about becoming a wealth accumulator.

Until you can live on 60% of your paycheck and apply the 60 / 40 principle to all your income, make a pact with yourself right now that you will apply the 60 / 40 rule to any money that comes to you that is not your paycheck. This means any bonus, rebate check, birthday money, raise at work, money on the sidewalk, whatever; you get the idea. If money comes into your life in any form but your paycheck, apply the 60 / 40 rule to it.

It is amazing what happens to my clients as they do this. First of all, I have to convince them that their penny jar is a powerful technique for opening the flow of money. Most of them laugh at me. "You're kidding, right?" is a common response. No, I'm not! Do it today. Most of my clients did do this one action item, and they achieve immediate and incredible results. Many of them tell me in later phone calls, "Janine, I thought it was the stupidest thing you had asked us to do. I knew it wouldn't work. Then I got a rebate check in the mail." As soon as they

75

split up their money and put it into the different accounts, I began to get e-mails telling me of money that was coming into their lives. Checks were arriving from insurance companies telling them there had been an overpayment on their premium. (Yeah, right! An *overpayment*! Returned from an insurance company? We truly live in an age of miracles!) They were finding money on the sidewalk (one lady found a $20 bill blowing around a parking lot). One family finally sold a car after six months of unsuccessful advertising. One woman told me how she finally balanced her check book after 12 months of letting it slide and found she actually had $600 in her account over what she thought she had. I have no idea what way the Universe will choose to place money into your hands, but I do know that if you start applying the 60 / 40 rule to every dime that is not your paycheck, you will begin to see a change in your financial situation for the better. You will still have debt, but you will also start to see an increase in your savings accounts while you continue to pay down your debt.

This small example of progress toward wealth accumulation will give you the strength to implement the 60 / 40 rule for your entire paycheck once you have retired your debts. And that's when the Universe really starts to funnel money your direction! So start now, and prime the pump so you get on with building real wealth!

Handling Your Current Debt Load

Speaking of debt, what is your current debt load? Do you know it? Do you know what you owe to the penny? Mary Hunt's story provides wonderful inspiration for staying out of debt. Read her book, *The Complete Cheapskate*. I like her very sane way of handling debt you have already accrued and yet making peace with the past and getting on with your life. It took Mary and her husband 14 years to pay off the debt that she managed to amass. She takes total responsibility for it, but the reason it took them so long was that they decided that her husband didn't make enough money, so they started their own business – which failed. She states that they probably could have done it sooner if they had decided to let him stay in his job while she focused on decreasing their expenses. That is why the focus of my book is reducing your expenses rather than taking radical new approaches to getting more income. Don't take desperate risks to retire your debts. Instead, accept them and start to steadily pay them down with money saved by cutting out unnecessary expenditures. You know, the daily coffee and muffin at

Starbuck's rather than your own home brew, the full-price movie tickets instead of matinee, the new car rather than a low-mileage used one. The few coins in your jar can work dramatically to get money flowing into your life if shared out using the 60 / 40 principle. Now you can add to that store by not spending coins in the first place on items that you don't really need.

You need to come to grips with your current debt. I want you to list every credit card, medical bill, student loan, car loan, boat loan, personal loan, and house payment and record the balance on each. This is the single biggest issue that is keeping you burdened, that is keeping you from being financially free. This is what is keeping you up at night, and what is causing much of your stress. You don't have an accurate handle on your debt load. So list every single debt you owe and then the balance you have on each. That means break out all the statements. You thought your obituary was tough. This one exercise, if you have large credit card debts, can bring a person to tears.

For those of you who don't have any credit card debt, put your car payment and your house payment on there and see what you can do to pay them off as quickly as possible. Why? I want you to be financially free! I don't want you to owe a debt to a single person except yourself.

Do the Math!

One gentleman asked me during a seminar, if you only have one debt and that is $90,000 on your house, how do you set up a reward system for that? I answered by getting the room to applaud. If you don't have credit card debt and the only money you owe is on your house, then I say three cheers for you! I'm jumping up and down here in celebration for you. Do you realize how many people come through my door in financial need and don't know what to do? Very few are that free of debt. If the only debt you have is a house, really look at your situation and figure what is the best benefit – paying it off early, or investing the extra payments in something else (like a retirement account).

How do you decide? Do the math, of course! Do you plan on living in that house the rest of your life? If the answer is "yes," I would say pay that puppy off as fast as possible. One good way to accomplish this is to use the idea from David Bach's book, *The Automatic Millionaire,* where you make your house payment every two weeks. Bach has provided a list of companies that you can use for this service, or you can do it for yourself. Pay it off as fast as you can because then you are debt-free and you can get on with your purpose – all the while directing those former house payments to the service of your purpose. If that is not your situation and if you are going to move from your house in the next few years, then just figure out how much equity you want in the house so that when you move to your next place you can buy your new house with cash. See the difference here?

Now, I'm not an accountant and I'm not a financial planner; many of them will argue on this point, suggesting that prepaying the mortgage while skimping on investments is not a good way to build real wealth. I'm not talking about dollars and cents here, people. I'm talking about psychological well being. In order for you to feel like a wealth accumulator, you need to own what you have. Accountants and attorneys are looking at tax advantages and legal issues. Their perspective on this is totally different, except for the ones who are financially independent. If your financial advisors (and you should have some!) are financially independent, they totally understand what you mean when you tell them you want to experience the psychological joys of being debt-free. But it's surprising how few of our financial professionals actually choose to become wealth accumulators in their own right.

Debt is a funny thing. It is an emotional issue as well as a monetary one, an issue that attacks the very core of our well being. Every one is willing to give you advice on the subject. You're also going to get conflicting opinions. Please think about where the head (and self-interest) of the person is who is giving you the guidance. If the individual is talking about tax exemptions or advantages to being in debt (by having a home that you're paying interest on), ask them to prove it is an advantage by using *mathematics*. Do the Math! Crunch the numbers and see if you really do have a benefit. Use emotion in the service of reason here, and you are more likely to get a good start on wealth accumulation and peace of mind.

Chapter 5:

Pay Yourself First

Let's discuss the power of saving over spending. The lifestyle put forth in this book is naturally unconventional in this day and age, and I'm asking you to be somewhat of a rebel. We're going to do things differently from conventional wisdom. My job is to assist you with problem solving. To help you to see beyond the quick fix solutions of "throw money at the problem." I want to help you get rid of the mentality of the quick purchase rather than to wait and barter for what you need or to buy something used, or to not buy it at all.

One of my favorite quotes about saving comes from Amy Dacyczyn. She comments, "A natural aspect of tightwaddery is the practice of unconventional methods to save money."

I'd like to tell you a story about a client of mine that perfectly demonstrates this quote. I had been mentoring people in the fine art of wealth accumulation for about six years. I knew by this time that teaching the principles of debt-free living was my purpose here on the planet Earth. I knew that whoever walked into my office, no matter the problem, I would be inspired in some way to help them. You can imagine my surprise when I had a client named Barbara enter my life. Barbara was an interesting individual because she was a mail carrier and she made $70,000 a year in Ventura County, California. She was filling my box with mail one day and was commenting on the fact that I was there every Tuesday to greet her. She asked, "What are you waiting for anyway?" I replied, "The grocery store circulars!" She was dumbfounded; she had never heard that one before. She had heard a lot of reasons for meeting the mail, but never that one. I was explaining to her a little bit about grocery shopping with a price book and how to lower your food bill and she said, "I have a real financial need." I said, "Really? Well, come by my office and we can chat over tea. I might be able to help you."

Two days later, she came by my office (okay, kitchen, but work with me here) and brought her financial statements, and it was my turn to be dumbfounded. She had a gross income of $70,000 a year and yet had zero disposable income. No wiggle room whatsoever. I had never seen any such desperate fiscal situation in my life. She was a single mom with two teenage sons. What had happened to her? She had acquired the habit of regularly getting advances on her next paycheck. You know those check-cashing places? I've never used them, so I was unfamiliar with the system. An interesting point about them; if you declare bankruptcy you still have to pay them. They charge anywhere from 22% to 38% interest on the cash advances. She needed cash so badly that she would go to these places two weeks or three weeks before her paycheck was slated to arrive, so she managed to get further and further behind. I don't understand all the workings of how all that happened. I was just blown away that she had zero disposable income.

Hard Choices

I sat there for a moment thinking, "Wow, I have nothing to offer this woman!" Off the cuff I happened to say, "You know, if you didn't have to pay rent, you'd be okay!" She sat there for a minute and she said, "I've got it!" I said, "Really? Educate me, because I have no idea how to get you out of this." She said, "I'm moving into a woman's shelter and I'm taking my kids with me. I'm going to stop paying rent, move into a shelter, and pay off my debts." She gave me a big hug, and said, "Thank you, Janine; you've been such a big help." She walked out of my office. Six months later, I am in a part of town I had never been in before and I see a mail truck parked on the side of the road with a woman eating lunch under a tree in the park. I immediately pulled around on the off chance that maybe it was Barbara. It was. I said, "Barbara, its Janine. How are you doing?" She told me that in six months she had paid off all her loans. I don't know how much she owed. I don't know any details, but she had managed to find an apartment with a lower rent, her two sons had started working, and the three of them were working for each other to get college degrees. They were tired of the on-the-edge lifestyle and they were now out to improve themselves.

So when I focus on being unconventional, you may have to become strikingly unconventional depending upon your financial situation and the goals you've set for yourself. I'm hoping that everyone who reads this book has disposable income. That you have something here for us to start with. But even if you don't, despair not. There are always options available. I encouraged Barbara to look into getting aid from the Women, Infants and Children (WIC) service, food stamps, and asked her to stop into her local food bank for nutritional support. She had changed her behaviors and she was moving in a positive direction. I love Barbara's story because it demonstrates that you sometimes have to be pretty radical to get what you want after a series of bad financial choices, and that there really is a light at the end of the tunnel once you make the hard choice to start doing the right thing.

Pay Days for Stay-at-Home Moms

This is a bit of coaching for stay-at-home moms. One of the biggest challenges for us, especially if we drop out of the work force to raise our family, is this: we don't get a paycheck for what we do. Or do we? I once sat down and figured out how much I would have to make a year at a corporate job in California in order to receive an additional $10,000 in take-home pay for our family. With business attire, day care, and no time to cut expenses, I would have had to earn $65,000 a year! Just think of the stress. There is such a cost to having two people out of the home and working. If you ever need a reminder that being a stay-at-home mom is a good thing, I suggest that you read *The Two-Income Trap* by Elizabeth Warren and Amelia Warren Tyagi. This book will help you realize just how much money you're saving by "working" from the home. Amy Dacyczyn discusses in *The Tightwad Gazette* the concept of an hourly wage based on how much money she saves rather than earns. For example, by spending 45 minutes to make three phone calls to different insurance providers, she saved $600 on car insurance, which calculates out to an hourly wage of $800 for the time spent. Yes, we stay-at-home moms really can "earn" more by working hard to save money. By staying home and promoting behaviors that keep your family from spending money unwisely, you're moving into the elite of America by being a conserver. That is the philosophy we are going to discuss in our consideration of the Pay It Forward principle (Chapter 6).

Easy Ways to Save Money

I've added fresh research data and comments from seminar participants to show you the shift in our thinking as consumers since the 1970s when Joe Dominguez and Vicki Robin wrote their book, *Your Money or Your Life*. These

"Sure Ways" will immediately make a difference in your cash flow. All you need to do is implement them.

1. Don't go shopping

In *How America Shops™ 2002*, the eighth study in a series published by WSL Strategic Retail, recent surveys show that in the last decade there has been a slow but steady rise in the number of weekly trips people make to go shopping. In 1995, researchers noted that participants were shopping 1.7 times per week. By 1997, the number of trips had increased to 2.5, with today's numbers topping at 4.5 times per week. With this increase in exposure to marketing snares and opportunities for impulse buying, the temptation to far exceed our needs is too great for most of us. We begin to fall prey to perceived needs created by our consumption-based society. To avoid an undue shift in your internal barometer of needs, avoid shopping as entertainment, socializing, or as a means of simply killing time. Because of this increase in shopping trips as a social event, marketers have coined a new term to describe *their* favorite customer behavior: "shoppertainment." You want to sincerely shun every opportunity to be a member of this group.

2. Take care of what you have

I get this from the men that I mentor. "But I really need this new (put power tool of your choice here)." Okay, why? "It can do (list 100 different options here) that my old one can't!" "Okay, how about you rent one?" Ah, the light bulb comes on. We are so programmed by our long experience in capitalism and immediate gratification to just go out and get the next widget that we totally forget to rent or try borrowing one. We do not need to own many of the tools required for home maintenance or landscaping. Take this spring's decision that Brad and I made as an example.

We were preparing to put in a garden. The last thing we were going to do was go out and buy a tiller, despite the fact that the piece of ground we selected hadn't been used before for growing vegetables. We were going to go rent one for a couple of days. That way we don't have to store it; we don't have to maintain it; we don't have to buy it; and we don't suffer from buyer's remorse or tiller envy. All we do is use it, put some gas in it, and return it to the rental store. This works equally well with transportation. Many times I've been able to coach people that have two cars to drop one car payment by renting the second vehicle only when you need it. I mean, Enterprise

Rent-A-Car will even pick you up!!! You don't have to worry about how to get back and forth to rent the car.

3. Wear it out

You already think this way in terms of your clothing. Now start thinking like this in terms of your house, your car, appliances, and other major expenditures in your life. If you're going to buy, make it worth your while. Make sure it is something you really need, and then buy it and wear it out. You will then be getting true value for your money. If an item costs you $300 and you use it for 10 years, then it only cost you $30 a year. This is a really good return on your purchase price. Bought in this fashion, your stuff almost assumes the character of a true long-term investment. To get the best value, spend a little more up front to obtain items of high quality – and then maintain them regularly to extend their life for years. Brad and I buy new cars, which are obviously quite expensive relative to used ones. However, we know all the foibles of the weirdo owners and the exact details of the vehicle's history. We can justify the cost because we keep them for fifteen to twenty years. Averaged over that much time, the original purchase price yields a quite low cost of annual operation for a reliable and well-maintained vehicle.

4. Anticipate your needs

This is part of the Short-Term Savings account. If you anticipate what you are going to need in the near future and you start looking into the potential purchase price of the item now, even if you don't have the money for it, even if you can't buy it today, amazing things will occur. You will find somebody who is trying to get rid of said item and you will be able to buy it for 25% of what you were willing to pay for it. If you write out your wish list for the year's expenses, you'll be much farther ahead. There is a wonderful Canadian named Charles Long who wrote a book called *How to Live Without a Salary*. One of the neat things about Canadians is that they are exceptionally frugal on the whole because of their strong sense of environmentalism. If you want a really fun read on Canadian philosophy of frugality that is different from the American perspective, I would recommend this book. Why? Because Long talks a lot about the barter system and how to use your community to support one another in your frugality efforts. How you tell people what you need so that you actually get responses back. I had one client who used such techniques to get low-cost housing, dental work, and business equipment.

5. *Think about how you'll use it*

Amy Dacyczyn talks about the purchase of a teapot versus a sauce pot. One item can perform only one function (boil water for tea), while the other has multiple uses. Save space, save money and get the pan. Ask a toddler to show you how to use items in unique ways if you need inspiration!

Instead of buying a new widget that you think you need, ask yourself if there is something that you already own or can borrow that will do just as good a job. My eldest son loves the woodworking shows on public television; Norm Abram and *The New Yankee Workshop* is a particular favorite. Have you seen this show? I mean, this guy has tools for everything! My son is constantly remarking, "Oh! Mom! Can we buy one of those?" I say, "Honey you have a hammer, a saw, screwdrivers, and some sandpaper. That is all you're getting for a long while!" I already have to work with my children on the multiple-use aspect of tools and the philosophy of reasoned rather than impulse purchases.

6. *Get it for less*

You may be one of those folks who could tell me all about bartering and the fine art of horse trading. I love going to yard sales in the southwest because people are used to haggling. When I lived in Japan that was how my mom would buy groceries; you haggled, you never paid full price or the shopkeeper was insulted. Americans rarely haggle when buying stuff. We think our time is too valuable and we don't take the time to work the price down.

Even when I lived in Los Angeles, if I needed something, I would see if I could be successful at haggling. Occasionally, I was in for a surprise. Once I was helping a friend of mine buy a patio set. I was mentoring her in the fine art of the haggle. I walked up to the store manager and said, "I like that patio set you have there. Is that your last one?" "Yes." "Oh, that's too bad. It's not in a box. I don't know if I have a truck that can haul that. Would you take 15% off the sticker price since it is already put together?" The guy bought my line. It was already put together you'd think he would want *more* money for it. He replied, "We don't do deals here. Tell you what; I'll give you a flat $75 off." I agreed and paid the money. What he didn't realize was that from the $399 sticker price 15% was going to be $60. He basically said "I won't haggle" to me and took $75 off. Now supposedly the idea is to get the customer to pay more, not less! We're so lazy mentally with math that if you can do simple percentages in your head and make offers on the spot you can sometimes come out with great deals. Even if you only succeed in getting a small reduction in price, haggling is a worthwhile practice because every little bit helps as you try to accumulate wealth.

7. Buy it used

When I mention this section in my seminars, people immediately think of thrift stores and clothing, but for some reason their brains shut down on other things. With the invention of EBay this point is not the radical concept it seemed to be in the 1970s and 1980s. EBay has really changed this viewpoint, and now you have to be careful because some companies have designed new products for specific and regular selling on EBay. There is a whole psychology that is happening with on-line auctions. Just think of professional auctioneers at work. You know their fast talk is meant to promote a fever of rapid bidding without thinking to get the sale price way over the sane price. The last three to four minutes are the most furious. I recommend you go out and look up how much your item would be if you purchased it brand new before bidding on EBay – and then lower your highest bid amount by 15% and remember to include the cost of shipping. I don't know how many times I've been able to get a new item cheaper from an online or local store then I could get it on EBay using this method.

How to Rein In the Impulse Buying Monster

Everyone knows what their own passion is. There are certain events, places or situations that get you excited about buying. I am going to outline fourteen simple questions that I want you to ask yourself before you initiate any major purchase in the future. I often laminate this list and hand it to my clients so that they can keep it ready at hand in their wallets when shopping as a ready reminder to stop spending their life away. Brad and I go through this list for any item over $50. We'll sit down and have a little meeting on the proposed purchase. It takes us all of 15 seconds to five minutes depending upon how far down the list we have to go and whether we need to have a serious discussion. You set your own limit. You know in your own family what would be appropriate for you. We were trying to become financially independent in 14 years, so we were really watching the money that we were spending. I remember a phrase used by Brian Tracy when he would discuss tips on being effective in life. He says, "Elephants don't bite, mosquitoes do." This is a wonderful pictorial representation of how our much small expenditures rather than the few big-ticket items will maim us on the path to financial independence.

Paying With Cash

Take, for instance, the Bolon family discussion about the need to purchase a second vehicle. Up to the arrival of our fourth child we were fine with one vehicle (as Brad walked to work). However, our truck only held five people, and we were now to become a family of six. We had to go out and buy something that we had been dreading for years: a minivan. Ugh! We searched. Let me tell you, I scoured dealerships for six months, essentially the entire time that I was pregnant, for any vehicle other than a *minivan* that would hold six people comfortably and meet some other needs we had. The Chevy Suburban came close; unfortunately, it didn't have as much storage space or as easy access to the rear seats, and it used a lot more gasoline. I would walk onto a lot and ask the eager sales person, "Do you guys have anything that will hold six people comfortably, stores luggage, gets decent gas mileage, and that can take us off-road camping in safety that isn't a minivan?" After their grin subsided or their laughter faded, they would politely say, "I'm sorry, but no." After we found the vehicle we wanted (and yes, it was a minivan!), I went on line and had car dealers bidding for my business. We finally got a very good price on a Honda Odyssey. We decided on the program car at one particular dealership. The program car is used by dealers for the test drives. We waited for the new models to come out and bought the previous year's program car. They detailed the van, gave it a full tune up, and it had something like 185 miles on it. We were able to pay cash for this vehicle. You should have seen the salesman's face as we walked in with our four kids and said, "Yes, we would like to pay for this in cash." That dropped the price by almost $6,000 and we got a cargo net thrown in for free (a $250 value at the time). When you walk in with cash, it is quite a convincing medium of exchange. We made this purchase with a figure of exactly how much we were willing to pay. I still don't like being a minivan owner, but knowing we got such a terrific deal on this easy-to-maneuver van makes the pain more bearable!

Ask Before You Buy

Okay, let's go through the list of 14 questions you will need to be asking yourself before you complete any major purchase. Why? Because you'll save money in the short term, and that builds real wealth for the long haul. These questions are:

1. Can we do without it? Do we REALLY need this?

2. Does it do more than required?

3. Does it cost more than it's worth?

4. Do we have something that will do just as well?

5. Is there a cheaper substitute?

6. How often will we use it?

7. Where will we store it?

8. Will using it be more work than we want to do?

9. How many ways can we use it?

10. Have we checked with people who own one?

11. Can we borrow it?

12. Can we rent it?

13. Would my hard-earned money be better applied toward another goal?

14. Should we wait? – Yes, ALWAYS! 24 hours at least!

Now let's go over the thought process behind these 14 questions one by one.

1. Can we do without it, and do we really need this?

If you ask yourself, "Do I really need this?" and you hesitate longer than two seconds, you don't. Move on. Stop looking at the item; if necessary, leave the store. Some marketing tool rather than a real need is motivating you to buy this thing. I emphatically suggest that you invoke a goal affirmation as you walk away to realign your vision with the emotions you're experiencing. Establish why you are not in true need of this product. Don't work on justifying why you need it. Instead, clarify why you don't need it. You will feel better about yourself, trust me. My guess is that something has happened in your life and you are trying to fill the gap with a purchase. Get away and go analyze it. What is the true need that you are trying to fill with a quick fix? Was it the argument with your husband? Was it the bickering of your children this morning when you had only had two hours of sleep? Are you just plain depressed? Find a way to heal yourself without using money to buy something you don't really need. The thrill of buying is nothing compared to financial freedom.

2. Does it do more than is required?

This goes right along with the Bolon family purpose statement. We are always working to be as simple as we can be. If an item can do more than we need, we constantly look for the simpler model. This is not easy; especially when it comes to technology. Have you tried to buy a DVD player lately? Or a television? It is like ordering a private jet, there are so many options and buttons and ways to interface with everything from your computer to your toaster. It is amazing what happens when you ask sales people for simpler models. We wanted to get a new CD player because our old one was damaged in a move. I walked up to the salesman and asked, "I'm looking for something that can hold five CDs and doesn't talk to me. I just want a *very* simple CD player." He goes, "Oooo, you must be a computer-phobe." "No," I calmly replied, "I just want something simple that doesn't have a display screen like the space shuttle." His response was classic. "Well, yeah, that is going to be tough. But we have something like that in the back in the scratch-and-dent department that I can let you have for $25." I was shocked it was so inexpensive and almost shouted, "What? Sure, sold!" I got it home and it was still like the space shuttle, I regret to say. I actually had to break out the book to set the clock.

However, I can assuage the mental trauma because of the marvelous discount.

3. *Does it cost more then it is worth?*

Some of these questions are going to be "no-duh" types to you at first glance. But remember what we are trying to do here. We need to slow down the process of our thinking so that we can change our impulse reactions to the marketing tools being used in the various retail settings. These questions are psychological tricks to get you to slow down your response time in reacting to a perceived need. This way you have a defense and you don't get too excited by a salesmen's pitch, some slick marketing ad, or whatever. Also keep in mind that "worth" is a subjective thing. Some people might really value a $100,000 car because of the quality craftsmanship, or buy gourmet cheeses because of their exquisite flavor. If you are one of those people and such purchases give you true value, go for it. For the rest of us, however, our true measure of value lies in a $20,000 car and a home or college education or time spent with family. Worth is what YOU make of it. Just make sure that the price you pay really gives you value.

4. Do I have something that will do just as well?

I can't tell you how many times I've had a client tell me, "Janine, such and such has happened and I need to get a loan." My response to them is invariably, "You want to avoid that at all cost, because that increases your debt burden and we're working to get you out of it. Is there anything that you already have that you can use instead?" I just start mentioning options and I'm brainstorming with them on things that might serve their need as well. Frequently, the reaction will be, "Oh, I have something stored in my uncle's garage that will do this perfectly. Thanks, Janine," and they hang up. The problem with most of us is that we have so many possessions in our life that we don't know what we have. We buy four pairs of scissors over the course of six months because we can't find the old pair due to the huge amount of stuff we have stored in our homes. One classic example of this dilemma is related in Don Aslett's book *Clutter's Last Stand,* where he mentions that he had four identical pairs of vinyl work boots stored all over the place in case he needed them. And if he had had just one pair he would have always known where they were because he would have been more careful where he placed them. All four of his boots rotted due to disuse or poor storage, and he ended up having to buy a fifth pair which he kept in one location.

5. Is there a cheaper substitute?

This question seems self-evident based on the ones we have asked previously. Can you "get by" with a simpler CD player or bear to be seen in a less expensive car? For most of us, the answer is "yes" – if we actually take the time to consider the problem *before* we spend the money!

6. How often will we use it?

This is a good one. That was the primary question for the garden tiller discussion in the Bolon family. That was the real reason we weren't going to buy it. How often were we going to use it? We would use it once a year, maybe twice a year if I wanted to be really aggressive in my gardening. Another example is shampooing carpets. Why would you want to buy a carpet shampooer when you can easily rent one at the grocery store for a few dollars a day? And maybe once a year you have a professional come in and clean your house for you. If you have really expensive carpets that you don't trust to a rented machine then get a professional to shampoo your carpets for you. You'll still save money in the long run. Besides, you'll be helping someone else put their kid through college. Just think of it as a novel means of putting your money into circulation so that the Universe owes you something. Right?

7. Where will we store it?

This is a big problem in America, Canada and England, These three countries have serious storage issues. This is due to our high standards of living. One client family of mine was so excited over the amount of money that they had saved in four months that they called me up and said, "Guess what? We're going to buy an ATV!!!" (all-terrain vehicle) I said, "Oh really?! Wait a minute. Don't you live in a townhouse? Where are you going to store that thing?" They were so excited that they hadn't thought it through. If it is going to cost you money to store it, not only do you have the expense of the item, but now you have a monthly storage bill tacked on top of it. I know many of my clients have storage units. If you want a real hot business tip, invest in storage units. I am not kidding. It is a rapidly growing industry in America. I've lived in Cedar City, Utah for only two years and have seen three new storage businesses being built.

8. Will using it be more work then it is worth?

A good example of this is an electric potato peeler. I was blown away by this commercial. Not only were the motions required the same but it didn't really help you go any faster! Yet, here is an item that will now take up more space in your kitchen, and it will incur the additional cost of needing electric power as well. And even with all that, most of us would never get around to throwing out the old potato peeler!

9. How many ways can we use it?

This question is designed to help you get the most bang for your buck. Consider the purchase of that all-terrain vehicle again. For many of us, our only means of using it would be on the occasional trip to a national park. Not a good buy, but a fantastic opportunity to rent. However, others of us might have a real need for an ATV. Maybe your job takes you into the back country all the time (like my father, a professional gold panner, or a park ranger friend), or maybe you have a small farm and need a durable and fast vehicle for hauling or herding. If you can use the item in multiple ways on a regular basis, then it makes sense to buy it. Then you just have to take the time to find the best deal.

10. Have we checked with people who own one?

I love talking to people about, "Hey, how do you like your brand X minivan?" They either love it or hate it, and they can usually tell you exactly why. So when you're in the market for something, talk to people about their purchase. Do they like it? Does it have any quirks? Take cars, for example. One of my favorite things to do is to go by car dealerships and see what model of car is most abundant in the repair shop. It is amazing how you will see most of the cars at the shop on a given day will all be of one model. You can get the same feedback from magazines and websites that publish consumer ratings. The information is out there, and it will help you avoid buying that lemon. All we have to do is take the time to ask!

11. Can we borrow it?

This is a legitimate means of frugality. Find someone who has the item, and then ask to use it. This is an especially important way to see whether or not you really want to buy the item for your own use, because it helps you to avoid expensive mistakes. Borrowing something that you only use occasionally is a good means of getting your chores done for a reasonable price. And it builds community ties, because the people you are liable to ask first will be your neighbors. Brad and I are thinking of using this route with respect to the garden tiller. The only thing to remember is that you have to return the items you borrow. What's more, you have to return them in a timely fashion and in good order. That's right, clean them up, fill the gas tank, and offer to pay for repairs if it breaks while in your care. These minor costs are still going to be cheaper than buying something you don't really need, and the brownie points you gain by being a courteous borrower can build and cement good feelings in your community for years to come.

12. Can we rent it?

This is just another form of borrowing, and of keeping the garage uncluttered. I think we covered this enough in the questions above.

13. Would my hard-earned money be better applied toward another goal?

This question brings your purpose statement back into play. This is just another way of slowing our decision-making down, by having us make sure that the thing we think we "need" is really a need and not just a want. This question answers in the affirmative if you even hesitate while reading it. In that case, put the cash back in the wallet (because we don't use credit cards, do we?) and move along.

14. Should we wait?

Yes. ALWAYS! Give yourself at least 24 hours from that first impulse to buy before you actually purchase anything. Why? This gives your brain time to come up with alternatives. It also gives the Universe time to help you by motivating other people to talk to you about the item you're looking for. If you are in the market for a new table saw, start asking everyone you know if they have one they would be willing to part with. You may think this sounds crazy, but I've used this technique time and time again for different appliances and gadgets, and I've been over 90% successful at finding what I needed at a much lower cost then I could have found at a store. Many times the item had never been used or used only once! The idea here is to limit your acquisitions to stuff you really need, and to only buy after due deliberation. After all, the name of the game is to keep *your* hard-earned money in *your* pocket.

Chapter 6:

Pay it Forward

This is the section on Saving. You know, good old-fashioned thrift.

Saving for tomorrow is the one best way for most of us to actually take control of our finances and future today. This is such a simple concept, yet a very powerful one. Not exactly rocket science, is it? *So why don't more of us actually buckle down and save?*

Recent surveys show that only 2% of Americans are savers, and the average savings rate is 0.4% of income. Imagine that! If you want to make a single step into the financial elite of America, this is the one! Just begin to save! Start saving your money and you become a minority, but a financially healthy minority!

Let's look at a real world example. A *Wall Street Journal* article (May 5, 2005) entitled *For the Wealthiest*

1%, Borrowing Can Pay Off reveals that the top 1% of Americans (those with a net worth of over $5.9 million) control 33% of the nation's wealth and hold only 6% of the nation's debt (mainly in their capital investments). In contrast, the bottom 90% of the country controls 30% of the wealth, but carries over 70% of the debt! And much of this debt amounts to taking out loans (by using credit cards) at high interest rates to buy stuff now – the exact opposite of saving for the future! Yikes! That leaves the 9% of Americans in the upper middle class, folks that have a net worth of $1 million to $5.9 million, in control of 27% of the wealth but holding only 24% of the debt (and that is mostly in their homes). It looks something like this:

Figure 3:   The Relation between Worth and Debt

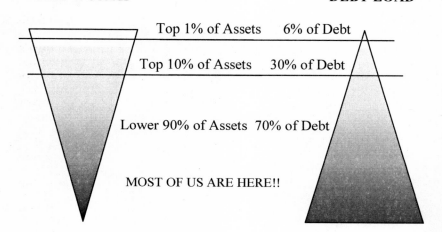

There is a direct correlation between having a nest egg for the future (long-term savings) and financial peace. (Again with the "No duh!" statements.) In my research sample of 33 families and nine single students (described in Appendix I, page 179), half of them had short-term saving accounts. The balances were modest, it's true, at just over $1,000, but at least they had them! In addition, 57% of them had long-term savings as well. Bonus! Obviously my sample is terribly skewed when compared to the national average! But in this case it pays to be part of the non-conforming group. Their efforts to save reveal that these families recognize the importance of saving.

This recognition is even more impressive given that the standard message delivered by modern society is that saving is, at best, a waste of resources ("don't delay gratification") and is, at worst, unpatriotic. Don't believe that last remark? Well, think about it. When the stock market tanks or a recession hits, what do the nation's leaders say is the means to the fastest recovery? They rely on the spending power of the American consumer to power the economic recovery engine of this country, and to a large extent that of the entire world. What ever happened to the mindset that saving was a means of serving the country?! Maybe we can't save the country all by ourselves, but we can start saving to save ourselves – and then we spread the word.

Pay Yourself Twice

Okay, enough of the soapbox. Let's get practical.

By the 60 / 40 principle of financial independence, each family should have at least two separate savings accounts, one for short term use (a rainy day fund) and another for long term needs (a.k.a. retirement). Why two accounts? Because they serve different purposes, and the different purposes require different safety features to protect your savings. The good thing is that you get to pay yourself twice – once for now, and once for later!

The short term account is there as an immediate resource for two types of expenses. The first is the occasional big-ticket item, like property taxes and insurance premiums. The second is to help you recover from emergencies. How do you pay to have the water heater replaced? Use your credit cards? Get a loan from the bank? I think not! You want to have a store of cash laid by for this purpose, because cash on the barrel head often gets you more rapid service and even discounts from repair people. So where do you park this money? It needs to be safe and accessible, so the best place is a savings account at your bank. The money won't earn you much interest as it sits there, but the key here is to keep your principal absolutely safe. Once your bank account reaches $2,000 or $2,500, you may want to deposit the money into a money market fund or short-term certificate of deposit that earns higher interest. Why go through the torment of shifting you money? Because it will make 0.5% to 2.8% more than the interest you'll get from your local bank savings account. Add that amount up over a 40- to 60-year period and you will have added thousands of dollars in interest to your principle!

The long-term account is there to fund future projects. The usual items you save for here are retirement and education. In this fund, you want your money to actually be making more money for you, rather than just sitting there in case you need it. Here you have to balance the security of your principal with the need to take on some risk to help make the money grow. How much risk? That depends on you. Brad and I have taken our long-term account and split it into several sub-accounts, one investing in stock funds (both in the U.S. and overseas), another investing in bond funds, and another plowed into real estate. We have diversified in this way because each of these different asset types has a different degree of risk associated with it. If the economy is bad, we might lose some of our savings in one sub-account, but the other two might be growing at the same time. Over the long haul the amount we saved from our incomes grows much bigger thanks to the miracle of compound interest.

Compound Interest: A Slow but Sure Track to Wealth

Do you comprehend compound interest? If not, this is the time to truly gain an appreciation for it. The wisdom quoted by my grandfather's generation is, "There are those who understand compound interest and there are those who pay it." Resolve now to be the one who knows how to use it, rather than one of those who gets used by those who know how.

The keys to making compound interest work for you are to *save early* **and** *save often*! The information in Table 1 (page 114) shows you why. The case shown in the table is a simple one, where you receive a constant rate of interest (in this case, 6%) each year and never make any withdrawals. [Of course, the usual case is more complex, as you will receive a variable rate of interest depending on your investment choices, and it will be paid quarterly or monthly or even daily). Still, the table clearly shows what the wonders of compound interest can do for you:

Table 1: Make Compound Interest Work for You

Age	20 Year Old Invested	Grows to:	30 Year Old Invested	Grows to:	45 Year Old Invested	Grows to:
20	3000	3,180				
21	3000	6,551				
22	3000	10,124				
23	3000	13,911				
24	3000	17,926				
25		19,002				
26		20,142				
27		21,350				
28		22,631				
29		23,989				
30		25,428	3000	3,180		
31		26,954	3000	6,551		
32		28,571	3000	10,124		
33		30,286	3000	13,911		
34		32,103	3000	17,926		
35		34,029	3000	22,182		
36		36,071	3000	26,692		
37		38,235	3000	31,474		
38		40,529	3000	36,542		
39		42,961	3000	41,915		
40		45,538		44,430		
41		48,271		47,096		
42		51,167		49,921		
43		54,237		52,917		
44		57,491		56,092		
45		60,940		59,457	3000	3,180
46		64,597		63,025	3000	6,551
47		68,473		66,806	3000	10,124
48		72,581		70,814	3000	13,911
49		76,936		75,063	3000	17,926
50		81,552		79,567	3000	22,182
51		86,445		84,341	3000	26,692
52		91,632		89,402	3000	31,474
53		97,130		94,766	3000	36,542
54		102,958		100,452	3000	41,915
55		109,135		106,479	3000	47,610
56		115,683		112,867	3000	53,646
57		122,624		119,639	3000	60,045
58		129,982		126,818	3000	66,828
59		137,780		134,427	3000	74,018
60		146,047		142,492	3000	81,639
61		154,810		151,042	3000	89,717
62		164,099		160,105	3000	98,280
63		173,945		169,711	3000	107,357
64		184,381		179,893	3000	116,978
65	15,000	195,444	30,000	190,687	60,000	123,997

A 20-year-old who invests $15,000 ($3,000 a year from ages 20 to 24) at 6% interest will have a nest egg of over $195,000 by the time he turns 65. A 30-year-old investing a total of $30,000 over ten years ($3,000 a year from ages 30 to 39) at 6% interest has a nest egg of about $190,000 at 65. See the problem with delaying your savings program? Even a small delay means that you have to save a lot more to catch up. But let's say you've waited long past 30 years of age to start. Time and time again I have people look at the compound interest table below and compare it to their personal situation, and this glance just makes them depressed. They are trying to live a frugal lifestyle, they are over the age of 40, and they ask, "Is there hope for me, Janine?" As we can see from the table, a 45-year-old investing $3,000 a year until age 65 ($3,000 a year from 45 to 64, for a total contribution of $60,000) at 6% will reap a benefit of just a bit under $124,000. So don't panic if you have waited to start saving; compound interest will still work for you. Instead, go ahead and start investing now. It doesn't matter that some time has gone by. Starting late you won't end up with as much as the "save early, save often" crowd, but over $120,000 isn't chump change either!

If you save anything, it will beat what you are going to have if you don't start saving, which will be nothing! The biggest issue with compound interest is that most people's brains think of math in a very linear fashion, and compound interest actually is a logarithmic function (slow to start and fast at the end). As a scientist I have a good grasp on this concept because of all my work with bacteria and antibiotics. I'm used to seeing this type of non-linear growth curve since this is common in the natural world. This is also how compound interest grows. This type of investment is definitely not an instant gratification thing, but rather is one of those races in which the turtle that keeps moving at a slow but steady pace will eventually pummel the hare. It is the methodical, consistent saver who wins the race.

Saving Money and Priorities

About one week after my clients learn the 60 / 40 rule and go home to practice it, I start getting emails about what they should do with their money. Should they put this extra money to debt? Should they save? Should they do both at the same time, and if so how? Let's talk about the priorities of life and ways to save, pay down your debt, and still get a long-term savings account going.

117

Ask, Ask, Ask

We'll start by considering how to learn about money. I assume that's why you are reading this book, right? If you have difficulty understanding a topic, go and read three books on the subject. It doesn't matter what the topic is (money, in this case), and it truly does not matter which three books you choose. Just pick them, read them, and then think about them or discuss them with a friend. I have found with my own self-education that the third time I read a book on any given topic that my questions are finally answered and the whole subject clicks into place in my brain. The first time I go through a topic, I don't get it; it's challenging, and I don't understand it except at a superficial level. After reading a second book, my brain says, "I'm still fuzzy on this. I still have way too many questions." I read a third book and WHAM! It works for me. I've got it. Well, that's because I did all this foundational work with the other two. Read at least three volumes on a topic and you will assimilate the core concepts. (I've even given you some possible options in Appendix VI [page 193].) This is my recommendation to you, especially for your self-education on money and how to invest it.

Keep in mind, however, that learning about money is an ongoing process. The economy cycles over time.

New opportunities for wealth accumulation come and go. So once you have gained the basic understanding by reading your three books, keep up your education by reading magazines (*Money, Kiplinger's Personal Finance,* and *Smart Money* are the ones that Brad and I usually use) and papers (we use the weekly *Barron's,* the financial section of *USA Today* and sometimes the daily *Wall Street Journal* as our sources), and scanning financial websites. Remember, it's your money, and the best guardian for it will be you.

Don't let any subject, especially Math and Money, intimidate you. What you want to do in life is too important to allow ignorance of money to barricade you into poverty. Most of the math required to understand Money is simple arithmetic. No algebra. No calculus. No differential equations. It is all simple addition, subtraction, multiplication, and division. When my clients ask me nervously about their IRA accounts or 401k plans, like whether or not they should go with a traditional or Roth IRA, I always tell them to go talk to their accountant or their benefits department at work. These people get paid to know this stuff. Then after you get done chatting with them, if you're still confused, hit the books. Surf the web. David Bach's *The Automatic Millionaire* has an informative and easily grasped section on long-term savings. He also lists several mutual fund firms with investment options in many different asset classes (stocks, bonds, real estate, money market funds, etc.) along with their telephone numbers and web sites. I highly recommend that if you feel clueless about IRAs or even if you want a bit of a refresher, call three of the companies Bach has listed and ask them to send you an investment packet. Tell the good people on the other end that you know nothing about the topic and want information. It is in *their* best interest that you understand so that you will feel confident about depositing your money with them. They want you to feel secure when working with them. They will gladly help you. Many of my clients email me that they feel calmer about their finances after reading the literature sent to them. They feel more in control and can make informed choices on their accounts rather than just dumping the money and hoping for the best.

The primary aim of wealth accumulation is to take care of *you*. In particular, that you do the work yourself to take care of you. After all, if you don't make the effort to care for yourself financially, who will? Whose responsibility is it to make sure that you have enough money to last your whole life long? In your golden years, you don't want to be a burden to your children or to society because of your lack of planning. Take a few moments and commit to the responsibility of adulthood, which is take care of yourself first. Then you can go about helping others because you have handled your own needs accordingly.

Enter the Elite – Save!

The first question to ask yourself is, do you have any savings? If the answer is "yes," congratulations! You are in the top 2% to 3% of Americans. If not, it's time to get started. But how?

As always, you have options. Remember, you need two accounts, one for short-term needs and one for long-term dreams. The short-term savings account is simple. Go to your bank. Give them some money, or make a transfer from your checking account. Tell them to put it into a savings account. That's it. Continue to add to this savings over time using the 60 / 40 principle until you reach your comfort zone (about three months to one year of salary for most of us), and then leave it alone. Tap it when you have that occasional large expense or an emergency (and don't forget to refill it!), but otherwise just let it ride there until you need it.

For long-term savings, the simplest option for most of us is to start contributing to the 401k or 403b plan at work, because we can put money into the account each paycheck and end up doing so before we ever see our take-home pay. This approach is brilliant, because it's easy (the benefits department helps you with the paperwork), it happens regularly, it's completely automatic, and you don't miss money you never see. In short, it takes a one-time, up front decision to enroll, and then all the thinking and emotional hand-wringing is over. You're in, you're saving – and you're starting to build some real wealth!

Self-employed individuals get to choose between a variety of retirement plans, including solo 401k vehicles, a SEP-IRA, and Keogh plans. Again, accountants and mutual fund firms are just waiting to help you select between these options. If you can't take advantage of one of these accounts, then you will need to open a second savings account at your bank so that you can start saving to open your own IRA.

In fact, most of us are candidates for opening an IRA in addition to funding a 401k through work. Why? Because if you can afford it and meet the legal requirements, you can save even more money now, which translates into big bucks when it comes time to retire later.

Remember, the basic two rules: pay yourself first, and save early and often.

How does this work in practice? If you have a 401k at work and contribute 10% or more to it already, then your long-term savings account is off to a great start. If you can, contribute the maximum possible amount to your 401k (currently $14,000 a year), or at least to the point where the company matches your contribution (usually the first 3% to 6% of your salary). You may also wish to contribute to an IRA each year to keep compound interest working as hard as it can for you. This is especially true if you are over the age of 30. You will want to put as much money as you reasonably can into long-term savings for your retirement.

As for the short-term savings account, once it gets to $3,000 to $5,000 you may wish to make your money work a bit harder for you by placing it in a money market mutual fund at a mutual fund firm rather than your local bank. These funds at mutual companies usually make 0.5% to 2.0% above the interest rate offered at your local bank, and every little bit helps when playing the compound interest game. You may think at first blush that won't be much, but take that 2% increase and multiply it over a 20-year period and that can mean a real difference of thousands of dollars.

Saving a Year's Income

Now that both of these savings accounts are open, it is wise to start working toward saving enough money in your short-term savings account to cover six to twelve months of salary. Should you be unfortunate and lose your job or have an extended disability leave, having that money around will definitely calm some of your anxiety. After you have managed to gather that much cash, start working on your own education. To continue the wealth accumulation cycle, it is wise to continually increase your human capital as well as your financial capital. You have intellectual property that you walk around with between your ears (and we're talking accumulated knowledge, not ear wax). Keep it growing and energetic by continued self-education in your current profession – or in a field into which you would like to move.

Saving for the Children

After you have contributed the maximum possible amount to your long-term savings account, **and** you have accumulated funds equal to six to twelve months salary in your short-term savings, **and** you have enough money for your own education, **then** you can think about setting money aside for your children's education or financial needs. I'm not trying to be harsh here. I'm just trying to show you that *you must take care of yourself first* before you reach out to assist others. If you don't save in the proper order, one small financial crisis can move you into financial disaster. Besides, the kids are young. They have a lifetime of work ahead of them to help themselves. Brad and I will help our four children get started in college, but the responsibility for finishing the job through work or loans will fall squarely on them. And that's not wrong, because the life they will be living at that point is their own, and they will have decades in which to find ways to fund their own Visions. No one is responsible for funding your vision, but you.

Besides, your kids are going to have a major advantage that you didn't. You're going to teach them the 40 / 60 principle while they are young, and they will be way ahead in the financial game thanks to ingrained good habits and the miracle of compound interest.

Saving for the Parents

After the children, you may want to think about putting money aside for parental care. Do you have parents that need a bit of help? Well, after setting money aside for your own needs, you focus on your children's needs, and then you can work on what you may wish to do to assist your parents. This is a personal decision, but as far as priorities go, this is the most rational order to put it in. Why in this order? Because your children are the future, both of your family and the country, while your parents are the past. Sure, we should honor our parents, but we can't sacrifice our own financial well being and our ability to carry out our life's grand purposes by making up for the discrepancies of other individuals. Help if you can, but from a position of love rather than obligation.

Last of All, Some Luxuries

Last, but far from least, are your wants (what we call "luxuries"). Now that you are out of debt, have taken care of your own basic needs, have contributed to the well being of your children as well as Mom and Dad, continue operating by the 60 / 40 rule and occasionally allow yourself an opportunity to splurge. Everyone has a different want. Is it a new Mercedes sports car, a bass boat, a plasma screen TV, or an annual trip to Hawaii? When you have handled all the previous needs, now you can focus on the expensive "wants." But guess what? In my experience, once your financial house is in order to this extent, most of those wants will have fallen by the way side, and the few that remain are often relatively inexpensive because you have learned to get creative with your money. You now rent or borrow instead of buy. A want fulfilled using the frugal path is just as enjoyable as one served by buying – perhaps more so, as the wealth will still be accumulating.

Chapter 7:

Philanthropy

Now we move on to my favorite topic. What do you do with that 10% of your income that you give out in charity to show the Universe that you understand the Big Picture?

I chuckled when I read Groucho Marx's quote, "The secret of life is honesty and fair dealing. If you can fake these you've got it made." The whole point of the 60 / 40 lifestyle in building financial independence is definitely to "fake it until you make it." Think of yourself as a philanthropist even if you can give only $10 at a time. And just say to yourself, in a few years those donations are going to be $1,000 or $1,000,000. Okay, so that few years may be 20 or 50 years. I don't think we're going anywhere too fast, are we? We hopefully are going to make it through 20 years or more of living. If you're going to be

60 anyway, wouldn't you like to have a few thousand or million dollars that you can start passing around? So start thinking big. The way you start thinking big is by planning today for a big tomorrow.

Money Must Flow

This section is all about giving your money away. You have worked very hard for your money. There are a few of you who may resent the whole idea of having to become a philanthropist. However, I cannot stress enough that we are supposed to take care of our community if we expect the Universe to take care of us. The Universe gives us plenty of money for our own basic needs when we realize what our true needs are. Refer back to Figures 1 (page 51) and 2 (page 52). The Giving arm is just as important to the flow of money as the Living and Saving elements. Once we become frugal and set goals and understand that we have a purpose on this planet much different from our original self-centered perceptions, money begins to flow into our lives. At what rate and from which sources are totally defined by who you are and what you want to do with yourself. The way money will come to you is as individualized as you are unique.

The main point is that we are supposed to care for those who are not as fortunate as ourselves. You, for example, have been able to read this book, one that will place you firmly on the road to financial freedom (provided you implement the ideas, of course). But what about people who can't read this message? How many people in America are illiterate? In 1998, the U.S. government reported in *The State of Literacy in America* (released by the National Institute for Literacy) that "[o]ut of 191 million adults in the US, as many as 44 million cannot read a newspaper or fill out a job application. Another 50 million more cannot read or comprehend above the eighth-grade level." We have some excellent educators in this country, and they are concerned by these figures because they are on the rise. Not only that but it requires ninth-grade competence to understand the instructions for an antidote on a bottle of corrosive kitchen lye, tenth-grade competence to understand the instructions on a federal income tax return (some of us with advanced college degrees would argue that that is a low estimate due to personal experience, ahem, cough, cough), and twelfth-grade competence to read a life insurance policy. By the very nature of being able to read this book, do you see how truly wealthy you are in life skills?

So the point of philanthropy is to give money away. But do it knowing that you will benefit as much as the people who receive your gifts. Your acts of generosity invoke a reciprocal response from the Universe on your behalf. The saying "the more you give, the more you get" is totally true when dealing with wealth accumulation. Or anything else, for that matter. But be careful what you choose to give, because the Universe gives back in kind. Give clothes, and your neighbors will start dropping sacks of hand-me-downs on the doorstep. Give food, and fresh bags of fruit or vegetables come your way. So be careful what you choose to contribute. All charity is worthy, and will be rewarded both by good feelings and by material rewards. But if you want money to enter your life, you have to engage in real philanthropy and give your own hard-earned money away.

Obviously if you have a lot of debt, you've been living in a mentality of scarcity for a long time, and it may take you a few weeks or months to grasp that that the Universe has plenty of resources to send your way. So start small (remember that penny bank?) and work to bigger resources. Start remembering to give on a weekly basis. The 60 / 40 principle will help you get started in giving money away. As you start looking for organizations and groups to receive your money, people and organizations that need help will pop into your life, and you will realize that you can give away that electric skillet, that fourth cordless drill, that old toaster oven, or even a used automobile.

Holes in the Universe

But I'm getting ahead of myself, again. Let's back up a bit and discuss holes in the Universe. No, not black holes (although I would love to discuss it with you some time), but holes based on principle. As Evangelista Torricelli was becoming the first man to create a sustained vacuum in the 1640s, questions were being raised as to what was the "space" created as the mercury moved up and down in the glass rod? It was suggested that this was a vacuum. Such disgust was created in response to this correct explanation that we now have the English aphorism, "nature abhors a vacuum." This is a wonderful expression of the idea that any space left unfilled will be "unnatural" or go against all laws of nature and physics! Anyone who has a kitchen counter or desk that accumulates untidy piles of stuff will gladly assert that this concept is, indeed, true.

Why bring this up? Am I just trying to find another way to bring in my love for science and try to convert a few of you out there into this delightful field of inquiry? Partially, but I'm also wanting to show you how you can use this basic scientific principle to your financial advantage. I know this principle is true; whenever you open up a "space," the Universe scrambles to "fill" it. Ask any mother of toddlers with a once-clean living room floor. No matter how many times a day she may tidy the floor space, entropy will act through her offspring to produce the desired effect, chaos. The Universe seems to enjoy chaos, especially in the home, for everything always seems to be moving to clean surfaces, empty corners and unused spaces. Actually, chaos is not the goal of the Universe. It is balance. I know your experience may be to the contrary as you pick up the floor for the fifth time today. However, this is the micro version of this principle. Let's look at the macro version of what is going on. You created a space of order on your floor. The Universe set principles in motion (toddlers are perfect agents!) to balance the work (your effort) with work of your children (they, of course, call it play).

Clear Your Money Space

I promised that you could use this principle to your advantage. I recommend that you start giving away items that you no longer need. Also, if it is broken, throw it away. Dig through your closets, backpacks, purses, and drawers. Clean the basement and the garage. Take it slow and easy. Start with your purse or wallet. Move to your entryway closet, your bathroom cabinet and then on to the guest room closet, and finally, your master bedroom closet. Go through each room in your home and throw away or donate any item that you no longer need, that is broken, out dated, or thick with grime. Has it seen the light of day for the past five years? No? Then get rid of it! It is time for you to start creating some space in your life. If you don't make holes, flow will not be created. No movement can take place in a static space. Start the inertia required to get the Universe in motion *for* you. Ask yourself questions like, "How many shirts do I really need?" Look through what you have. As you get to t-shirt #15, make a decision, how many are you going to actually wear? I have learned that with my family I keep just enough clothes to cycle through the weekly laundry cycle. Actually, I do laundry six days a week. I learned that by doing small loads every day we needed fewer clothes then if I waited to do it once a week like my mother taught me. By this simple change in habit, I save us hundreds of dollars a year on clothes. Also, clothes have less time to sit and allow stains to really get stuck in them. I find that our clothes last a lot longer because I hang them to dry rather then using a dryer all the time. (Saves both money for the electricity and wear and tear while tumble drying, a frugal feast indeed!) During the winter months I often use our garage and during the summer months I always use our outdoor lines.

After you have decluttered your home, now is the time to start giving away the things you really do need – like money. Most people who come into my office need money. That is why I focus so much on giving money away. The more space you create, the more the Universe will fill it *in kind*. And it doesn't have to be just a physical space, like a closet. Give away "extra" money, and more will flood back in its place.

When the Universe Owes You

A great example of the Universe paying someone back *in kind* happened to me in January. I enjoy making blankets. I learned to crochet from a neighbor when I was nine years old and have continued learning the various nuances of the art. Quilts, afghans and blankets rolled off my hands over the years as I applied myself to these cottage crafts. Over the course of the last twelve years, I had donated 67 hand-made blankets to different charitable organizations. When the Tsunami Crisis hit southeast Asia in December, 2004, I felt so helpless, so miserable that I had so much and that these poor survivors had nothing left of the little they once had. I then started demanding from the Universe a way that I could respond to this crisis. What could I do *personally* to make a difference? I knew that giving away what you need works with money and I was now ready to test it on the blankets I had given away over the years.

So I organized a blanket drive in my county. I called schools; I presented my desire for blankets to local clubs and scout troops. Everywhere I went I talked about blankets and my desire to help the tsunami survivors. My goal was to have 500 blankets ready to ship in 30 days. People told me I was crazy. I was told that there was no way that the goal could be reached, not in the little town where I lived. But I knew it would work. I had created an obligation to me on the part of the Universe. The Universe *owed* me. This did not mean that I sat back and did nothing. Quite the opposite occurred. I set up meetings in my house where local clubs came together and assembled blankets in my living room from large donated fabric squares. I had quilt frames in every available space in my home and garage where people could crowd around and tie quilts. I called my neighbors. I called churches of every denomination and asked to speak to their members on Sundays. I looked in the Yellow Pages for quilt shops and thrift stores and asked them if they wanted to contribute something to the project. In the first three weeks of working, I had collected only 37 blankets. I continued to ask for fabric and gently-used blankets from people. Wal-Mart then had a sale on blankets and even more came in. After three and a half weeks I had amassed 244 blankets, a little less then half my goal. But I kept demanding from the Universe that it cough up its share of the quilts. On the last day of my campaign, a truck chugged up my driveway. Unknown to me, a student at a nearby college had heard of this project and had been gathering quilts as well. In that truck were seven huge boxes of blankets, which brought the total to 632.

A friend of mine heard this story and said, "God loves a photo finish!" I still smile when I think of that January blanket project. It was so Hollywood the way it came down to the wire. And yet, despite the last-minute delivery, the Universe and I met my goal, and we ended up sending 87 boxes of blankets to the tsunami relief effort. I don't expect everyone to believe me, but then, that's not the point, is it? I know this principle works, so I challenge you to test it in your own life. Don't just take my word for it. Try it yourself and enjoy life's miracles.

Just remember that the cycle returns to you more of what you have already given, so be generous with your money. Philanthropy is a major pillar upon which rests the eventual success of your wealth accumulation program.

The Law of Cause and Effect

This principle that the Universe will fill the Voids we create in our lives, and do so in kind, is well known. It goes by many names and is said in various ways. You've probably heard most of these depending upon your cultural or religious background. Some alternate versions are:

"The Law of Cause and Effect"

"The Law of the Harvest"

"What you sow, that you shall reap."

"What goes around comes around."

"Birds of a feather flock together."

"To him that has, more shall be given."

"Like begets like."

"Do unto others as you want them to do unto you."

Despite the near-universal acceptance of this well-known law, people still have difficulty implementing it when they need something or when they see that others are in need. With philanthropy, I want you to see yourself as unstoppable. When you're serving the needs of others it seems that the Universe goes to work overtime to get you what you need so that you can succeed. Yes, you still have to do your part and work like crazy while you move toward your goal, but you have to do that anyway, right? So why not rope the Universe into helping you out as well?

Remember, Sam Walton told me that one secret of success in business is to replicate yourself. This principle holds true for money as well. Sure, the Universe isn't one of your employees, but so what? A helping hand (or whatever the Universe provides) is still a helping hand.

My Empty Vase

I have tested this principle in a variety of ways. Come on, I'm a scientist; curiosity is my life. I enjoy experiments and seeing if something really works like the world tells me it does. One such experiment I tried, totally for the fun of it, involved an empty crystal vase on my counter top. Brad and I had received this vase as a parting gift from some friends many years ago. After I had children, this beauty was put away in a closet very high up! However, I had learned that I would be giving a financial seminar in a few months, so I tested the notion that "Nature abhors a vacuum." I put the vase out on a counter and waited to see what would happen.

Over the course of six weeks I had many visitors. Frequently comments were made to me on how I could put glass beads in the vase to make it reflect the light more dramatically. Or maybe I could put artificial flowers in it to showcase its classic lines. Another recommendation was that I move it to the mantle place and put a small candle in the bottom of it. I even had one gentleman walk over to the vase and dump his pocket change into it. His remark: "It drives me crazy to see something so lonesome and bare!" I burst out laughing. I couldn't help it. I did nothing to attract attention to this vase. My counter top had items on it other then the vase. (Remember I have four children under the age of nine years; of course I have other items on my counter tops!) It just sat there empty for the entire world to see and it was filled.

Once you mentally have this principle down, you can use it to get whatever you need from the Universe. Money is the biggest resource that people request because it is the tool that drives our goals and dreams forward. (Or pays the debt that we've gathered.) It comes down to giving it away to get it back. So get going and give it up. I promise that you will be amazed at the results.

Give to Your Interests

People usually ask me, "Where should I direct the 10% I dedicate to philanthropy?" Pick a group or organization that is doing something that is in line with your purpose and give to them. What are you passionate about? What challenge of the Universe do you want to help solve? One of my clients was a college student and liked to give free flute clinics to youth. She found an organization that collected used instruments, refurbished them, and gave them out to school children that wanted to learn to play but couldn't afford instrument rental and lessons. She wanted to bring music into the lives of as many people as possible. Her philanthropic gift was contributing to the progress of her purpose within her community, with the added advantage of improving her own talent as well.

Another question I frequently get is, "What is the difference between philanthropy and charity?" For me, *charity* is any service or material good given away or donated, while *philanthropy* is almost exclusively about money. Your decision regarding your levels of charity versus philanthropy will depend on what you have to give and what you would like to attract into your life.

Exercise caution when it comes to donating to any particular group. Choose one in line with your purpose, but also make sure that it is reputable. I'd like you to try this first. Look for a 501(c)3 organization; 501(c)3 is just a section title from the U.S. tax code that defines a group that is a tax-exempt non-profit organization. They won't ever go public and they won't have shareholders. But these groups are out to perform some specific service or make a product for the community's good. Once you find a 501(c)3, not only do you get tax benefits for your donation, but so does the organization. (Please check with your accountant on this.)

A few years ago I used to give to a group called Doctors without Borders. This organization sends medical personnel to areas of high need due to war, famine or natural disaster. Doctors and nurses would donate their time to perform surgery, give health care and open clinics. These people would use their vacation time and pay their own airfare. The primary administrative costs for the group were employees to handle the scheduling of the medical personnel. For every dollar you gave, 95 cents went to medical supplies. That is a very good return on your philanthropic "investment" in my opinion. Anything under 6% is good in my book, but I encourage you to do your own investigation and set your own personal limit on an organization's administrative costs. We have all heard about the recent embezzlement scandals at some well-known philanthropic organizations. I recommend that you call the organizations that you are considering and visit their web sites. Find a contact number and request their financial statements. Tell them that you would like to start donating to their group, but you would like to know where their funding goes. What is interesting is that when you ask for their financial statements, you'll get more information then you know what to do with! One organization that I was visiting to determine if I was going to support it had a board member walk up to me with a stack of paper three inches deep and said, "Here you go; this is everything we are about." Bonk! It was much more then I needed to know, but I was impressed by their openness and vision. If you're still a little hesitant, then ask your contact at the organization, "Where are you going with this? What is your ultimate goal?" They will gladly tell you. When I asked the Happy Factory (a very special Cedar City charity) about their vision, the founder said, "We may not be able to make a toy for every child who needs one, but we're sure going to try."

The Better Business Bureau (BBB) has a sister site that is called www.give.org. This site lists hundreds of charities. Each is scored on a system that is defined on the site. The BBB discusses how to give, and they have pamphlets you can print out. When you get excessive mail appeals (because once you start giving, you're on everyone's list!), they detail how to get your name off those lists politely. They have a whole checklist on how to look into the different 501(c)3s, because sometimes tax-exempt for them does not mean a tax advantage for you. So, as always with things financial, it pays to do your homework up front.

Give Anonymously

When it comes to philanthropy as a whole, I emphasize giving anonymously when you can. Why? Because when you give openly, the accolades you receive are your reward.

But how do you give anonymously to organizations? Someone will have to sign the check, right? The point is you want the person who is ultimately receiving the assistance to be ignorant that the money has come from you. Charitable giving is tough to talk about because it is a very personal thing. Give to whatever you are passionate about. Maybe someone helped you out when you were down and now you want to start an organization that helps others out. Like the janitor that gave $2.3 million to the college where he cleaned floors. He never had a college education. He wanted to make sure that there were scholarships available for underprivileged kids so that they could have what he had not been able to afford when young. Whatever your passion is, start looking for charities that serve that purpose. I even give this advice to my students who are in college and have very little to no income. I tell them, "You don't want money to sit. You don't want it to be static. Start finding a charity and even if you have to write $1.34 checks twice a month, do that. Start your money flowing and you can start getting the Universe in your debt."

Inspiration from a Philanthropist

One of my dreams, or rather one of my 20-year goals, is that I want to create a foundation that will give out one million dollar endowments to social entrepreneurs. I used to work for a man that did that. I was employed at the time as a secretary for Kelly Temporary Services. I was working while I was pregnant with my first child. (Funny, I had trouble getting a job as a chemist while pregnant!) What was fascinating about being a temp was that I got to see all kinds of people and businesses. This one businessman that made a big impact on me in regards to philanthropy started the Partners for a Drug-Free America Foundation. I think you've seen the now famous commercial. "This is your brain. This is your brain on drugs. (See raw egg drop into very hot frying pan and cook, sizzle, and pop.) Any questions?" I didn't even know this was *the* guy. I was called up to work for a stint of three weeks. My job was to assist his secretary with the file *room.* My primary responsibility was to organize and maintain the filing room for all the charitable donations to which this philanthropist was giving. This was his personal money, not a corporate effort. I learned very quickly how to screen charitable organizations through that temp job. Even though I never met him, he impacted me greatly with the way he handled his philanthropic giving. I want to have endowments like that! I want the ability to give to causes I think are doing great things.

Family is not Philanthropy

A word of caution to you before I wrap up this chapter. Giving money to family members as your preferred outlet for your 10% philanthropy arm will quickly stop the flow of money through your life. Why? Because giving money to relatives is not part of the "taking care of thy neighbor" philosophy that true philanthropy embraces. Family are people we care for out of immediate love or self-serving motives. We help them because they may help us. If we give to our kin, the Universe feels no obligation to step in on our behalf because the family should take care of its own. The Universe only helps us if we step outside our family and give with no expectation of an immediate return.

However, recent comments from some clients indicate that in future seminars I will have to make this point a bit more baldly, because many of them engage in this behavior and then wonder why the money cycle has halted. Children (yours or someone else's) leaving for college or on religious missions, gifts to siblings and foster siblings, and supporting elderly parents are all activities that were sufficient to break the flow for these participants despite the warnings in the seminar and the subsequent mentoring phone calls. **Giving to one's family is *not***

philanthropy. Sure, there is a high psychological need to take care of one's family (however distant in miles or blood ties), often even before one's self or one's neighbor. Hence the desire by most folks to give their philanthropic gifts to benefit members of the family. However, by doing this, you break the cycle of money between you and the Universe. Instead of money flowing to you the Universe redirects the money to someone who understands the principle that "giving back" means "giving out." All five elements in the division of money – living, long-term saving, short-term saving, tithing and philanthropy (Figure 2, page 52) – must be implemented at the same time. If you wish to give to family, make sure such donations come from the 60% "living" portion of your money.

Chapter 8:

The Tools of the Trade

Do the Math!

This is the time to break out the calculators and pencils. I want to walk you through a few of the simple systems that I use to lower my family's burn rate (which is the amount of money we spend in any given month). We already discussed learning what your trigger points are that cause you to buy on impulse. Now we will focus on being frugal every day without feeling deprived. The focus you want to have in your financial life, and life itself, is simply, "What do I need?" Settle for that, no more and no less.

Let's take a recent situation of mine as an example. I was rapidly getting busier and busier as my consulting business took off, I was finishing my Master's degree, and my husband's travel schedule for his own consulting business was increasing. As I tracked our expenses, I saw

149

that we were now having pizza (our family's favorite fun food) delivered to the house three times a month. This was costing us $60! I analyzed why we were spending money this way and realized that I had other things that I wanted to do with my time rather than make pizza from scratch. So I was using this delivery service as a convenience due to the intensive nature of my life. I was assuaging my guilt over the frequent pizza purchases by adding a salad with dinner for my family, but this was addressing the symptom and not the real problem. What was I to do?

I set out to drop the cost of delivered pizza without giving up the convenience. One possibility was to serve it only to the adults, which would have cut the bill in half. However, the anguished shrieks of children at this proposal coupled with the fact that I would still have to make them dinner led me to drop that option. Instead, I found a local firm that prepared your pizza for you to pick up and bake at home. This dropped our pizza expense to $45 a month.

The next month I went to the grocery store and loaded up on a variety of pizzas. The only requirement I had was that the pizza had to be made with *real* cheese. My family tested the various pizza brands and agreed upon the best one for our tastes. This cost me $24 that month. Then after we had chosen a particular brand that we liked, I waited for it to go on sale and bought 30 of them at once! Yes, 30. (I have a freezer in the garage to hold such bulk purchases.) These pizzas were smaller then the ones we bought or made from scratch, so it takes two to feed my family. When you average out the new price, the cost for our convenience pizza had fallen from $60 a month to $15. When life slows down a bit, I'll go back to making pizza from scratch and the cost will drop to $9 a month. But for now, I don't mind splurging the extra $6 to keep my sanity. This is how you go about lowering your burn rate without deprivation. You still get what you want, but you do not have to work quite so hard for it! That's a good deal, right?

It is easy to calculate this stuff. I've shown the math below so you can see how easy the calculations are.

---

3 delivered large pizzas per month, with tip. $20 each.

   3 x $20 = $60

3 bake-at-home large pizzas with coupon. $15 each.

   3 x $15 = $45

3 grocery store pizzas of various brands $2 to $8 each

   3 x $ 8 = $24

6 store pizzas of preferred brand, on sale $2.50 each

   6 x $ 2.50 = $15

151

See? Not tough at all. You *can* do this kind of simple math. Get out your monthly expenses and see where you can plug a few holes in your financial ship today. Remember, elephants don't bite, it is the mosquitoes that do!

Examine Disposable Products

Sometimes you just have to change your buying habits in order to get the best value for your money. I had one client, Linda, tell me that she was having difficulty figuring out where she could cut corners in her expenses. After two months of tracking, she came to my office and worked through her monthly expense sheet. I asked her about her paper towel use. Linda would only buy one particular brand and she knew exactly how many rolls she went through a week. I showed her that she was spending $520 a year on paper towels alone. It looked like this:

4 rolls per week @ $2.50 each = $10 a week x
52 weeks per year = $520 annually

She was appalled! She said she could afford to buy a new dishwasher for that amount of money! This gave her the motivation to stop using paper towels. Immediately she went out and purchased a bunch of inexpensive linen towels. The initial investment was $12.64 for 20. Even with laundering costs she knew that she was saving huge amounts of money by not using paper towels anymore. Unlike the pizza example, the paper towels were an item that required a change in habits. She told me later that she got rid of (technically donated) all of the paper plates, plastic knives, forks, spoons, and styrofoam cups from her prior purchasing runs. She realized that the only reason she used the throwaway items was because she didn't like washing dishes by hand (Linda didn't have a dishwasher). She went to her local thrift store and spent $11.26 on new dishes and flatware so that she only had to wash dishes once a day. By the end of three months, she had cut her expenses on weekly items enough that she could use her saved money to buy a new dishwasher.

Another woman I advised had a burning desire to become financially independent. Liz stopped buying Kleenex brand tissues. She instead went to a local store and picked up a few packages of handkerchiefs, six for each family member. Each kerchief had the first initial of the family member's name monogrammed on it. She told me that she didn't see an increased incidence of cold or flu in their family with this practice, and that it taught her children responsibility for their own things. And yes, she saved several hundred dollars by this simple change in habit.

Look at what you are spending money on. Are some of these expenses on disposable products? Why are you throwing your money away with these things? Can you find another alternative that will serve the same purpose but not cost as much? Is there a habit that you could change that would mean an increase in savings for an item that you really want more? Refer back to your purpose statement and goals for inspiration on this.

David Bach writing in *The Automatic Millionaire* called this phenomenon "the Latte Factor," after the amount of money wasted in a year merely by indulging without thought in that once-daily (or more) cup of Starbuck's coffee. What is it that you are buying routinely but that doesn't represent a real need or even a desirable value for you? Many times the only reason we're buying these items is out of habit. Can these habits be altered to eliminate the expense entirely, or can we find a cheaper but just as effective alternative? Instead of buying your coffee from a coffee shop or an espresso machine, buy a thermos and carry your homemade gourmet coffee to work with you. The thermos will be paid for within a week! See the power of a calculator, pencil and paper?!

The Grocery Store Game

This is a wonderful tool to use to immediately and drastically decrease your family's burn rate. You will see a pronounced difference in your monthly expenses, specifically your grocery bill, faster by using this tool then by any other means that I can recommend. But it requires some really specialized, high priced equipment. What you will need is a three-ring binder. Then you can go out and buy an A to Z index to put in it – or get really frugal and make your own. And then fill the binder with three-hole punched notebook paper. The last item you will need is a pen or pencil. (Okay, I was kidding about the high priced equipment.)

What you are going to do is create your own price book. Amy Dacyczyn was the first author I read that described this system. Invest the 15 minutes a week required to get this program up and running and you will have a huge return on the time spent. Or, as we frugal types like to say, you will achieve a very high hourly wage for your effort!

The first thing you do is sit down with your ring binder (price book) and write down the most frequent items you buy and the prices that you normally pay off the top of your head. If you are like most of my clients, you will have no idea what you pay for most of your groceries. The next thing to do is to grab your store advertising circulars. Most folks get these in the mail or have a spouse or friend pop by the store on the way home to pick up the week's circulars. Look over each circular and put down the sale prices of the items that you would buy that week; the most highly discounted items (the "loss leaders," or items sold below cost to lure you into the store) and thus the best buys will be on the front and back pages. For my family, we're always looking for milk to hit a sale. My kids know that we won't pay over $2 a gallon on milk. So each week we scan the circulars and find milk on sale at one of the four grocery stores we have in town. If it isn't on sale that week, we don't buy it. The longest we have ever had to go without milk was two weeks. Because of our price book, I learned that our stores have milk on a two-week sale cycle. I buy enough milk to last us through the two weeks as we wait for the sale to come around again. You can do the same thing with eggs, bread, bananas, or any other staple that you can name. You just have to do a few minutes of homework each week to keep your price book up to date.

Let me show you an example out of my own price book. We'll use bananas as an example. I have it under the "B" index tab as the first page. (It is followed by

"Blueberries" and then "Bread.") I give each item its own page, and that keeps things simple for me. I usually label the item I am recording on the top right hand corner of the page to make it easy to find. Below is what I recorded over a six-month period for "Bananas" after I moved to Cedar City. As you scan the table below, you'll notice that the prices go steadily down as time marches on and I have more purchases to compare:

Bananas		
Date of Sale	Store	Price / Pound
10/5/2003	Wal-Mart	$0.48
11/15/2003	Costco	$0.37
2/28/2004	Smiths	$0.35
4/15/2004	Lin's	$0.33

I only bother to write the prices of new purchases if they are lower then my previously recorded low price. What I am looking for are the trends used by grocery stores and their sale cycles. Prior to this six-month period, I had noticed that in general the four stores' average price for bananas was 59¢ a pound. (Occasionally, I would find prices like 65¢ or even 75¢ a pound!) My family buys bananas weekly, so this was a big expense. At the beginning of my six-month recording period, I found that our Wal-Mart Supercenter had a default price of 48¢ a pound. When bananas don't go on sale at the other stores we default to Wal-Mart to get our bananas that week. This saves us some serious money each year. What, you don't believe me? Watch, and be amazed:

56¢ – 48¢ = 8¢ a pound saved. Doesn't look like much does it? Well, it adds up over time to a substantial amount. Here is the proof:

8¢ x 3 pounds purchased in a week = 24¢

24¢ x 52 weeks in a year = $12.48 saved over a year

$12.48 x 10 years = **$124.80** saved in a decade

Still not impressed? Then think about this. All I have figured on this is the store that has the lowest average price. What about all the times I buy bananas when they are less than 48¢ a pound? What if I buy more than three pounds a week? Now, what do you think happens to my grocery bill when I do this with *all the items* that I purchase in a week? For 15 minutes a week, which is the time it takes to establish this price book and maintain a record of the sales price, I can save $900 to $1,500 (that is a conservative figure) a year on my groceries if I plan it right, depending upon how aggressive I want to be. Yes, I do end up shopping at multiple stores. But all of these stores are located within two miles of each other, so the cost in gasoline is minimal – especially if you do all your shopping on the same trip.

Let me give you a just a few examples of the staples on which I routinely save money, merely because I have a well-organized system for recording sales that allows me to shop only for the best-priced items and at the lowest-priced stores.

Savings on Grocery Items

Item	Average Price	Avg Low Price	Savings/ Item	Savings/ Week	Savings/ Year
Eggs	0.78/doz	0.59/doz	0.19/doz	$0.48	$24.70
Milk	2.63/gallon	2.00/gallon	0.63/gal	$1.89	$98.28
Bread	1.89/loaf	0.99/loaf	0.90/loaf	$2.70	$140.40
Bananas	0.56/pound	0.48/pound	0.08/pound	$0.24	$12.48
Total				**$5.31**	**$275.86**

These are just four items I buy every week when I go shopping, and yet I save almost $300 a year if I spend a few minutes a week finding the best deals. So for all those people out there who say it isn't worth the money to drive around to different stores I say, "DO THE MATH!" Even if I drive to three different stores to get my groceries in one week, I still have saved money. I can tell you that my car will not eat up $5.31 worth of gas each week (even at today's prices!) to make those side trips. Now take the savings that my family has for a year on just four items, $275.86, and multiply that figure over 10 years. That's $2,758.60, which is a fairly significant chunk of change! Do you think I'll ever stop buying these items? I don't think so. If anything I'll be buying them in larger quantities as my children develop into bottomless pits during their teenage years. Imagine how much you can save if you record most of the edible items (and, for that matter, the non-edible items) that you routinely purchase! You begin to see the power of this simple little tool, the price book.

My personal price book has 86 items that I track over time. Of that 86, I have intensively followed and tracked 28 of those items. These are items that I purchase weekly, or at least frequently when they are in season. The other 58 are there for a sort of reference. I don't buy them every week or even every month. When those items go on sale, I have a record of what "reasonable" is and I know if I need to stock up or not. Shampoo, Kleenex, and toilet paper are a few examples of these items. Seasonal items are corn-on-the-cob, strawberries, and cantaloupe. You get the idea.

Don't Forget the Good Book

To make this system truly effective, don't ever go shopping without your price book. I have advised my clients to buy a plastic business card sheet and put it in the front of their three-ring binder so that they can keep all their store-specific club cards and savings cards that the grocery stores gives them. I had one client tell me that she keeps her grocery money in a special zippered pocket she bought so that she *knows* she'll keep her price book nearby and won't forget to take it with her. Another client said she always keeps her price book in her car. She never drives anywhere without it. She uses her price book not only for her groceries, but also as a journal for generic products. The items that taste great were given a rating, as are the ones that were awful that she doesn't want to buy again. Her index also has a "Mc" tab. She uses this tab for tracking furniture she was shopping for and listing the stores, their phone numbers and the prices for various couches, coffee tables, and chairs she wants to buy when she has the money saved. I asked her if this was her version of a wish list. She replied "Somewhat. I know I'm going to get these things, so I'm comparison shopping and using my price book as my memory!"

Gorilla Grocery Shopping

Over the years I have heard and read all kinds of advice on grocery shopping. Most of them are scattered among a large number of books; some came from Internet websites. What I have done here is to list all the pieces of advice in one place for you. Take this list and practice it as you are able. Please don't think all of them have to be done at once. For the most part, I just want you to become aware of the $3 billion of marketing used per year to get you to buy stuff that you don't really need at all, or that you don't need at the time you are incited to buy it.

This is exceptionally true in the super stores and warehouse stores that are now so abundant in our landscape. This list is a guide and a caution to increase your consumer awareness. Let's take a simple example. Why do the warehouse stores have such large grocery carts? Consumer studies show that we have a tendency to slow our purchasing as we fill the space in our cart. Hence, stores supply larger carts at the warehouse clubs. I was shocked when I first read this piece of research. All this time I thought that the larger carts were for the gorilla-sized bulk product boxes. Silly me! Research has also revealed that most people, when faced with an option of turning left or right, will turn right. This being so, the aisles that you are more likely to go down first will have items that are smaller in size so that you have more room in your cart as you move along shopping. Again, the goal of our retailers is to get you to buy more stuff. Your goal is to buy only what you need and to pay as little as possible in doing so. Get the picture? Be especially careful in warehouse stores that you actually need to buy the items in such vast quantities. You only save money buying in bulk if you use all the stuff you buy, right?

Here is a list of tips to assist you in winning the Grocery Store Game.

Ways to Save and Be Aware
While Grocery Shopping

1. *Use a price book.* Thank you, Amy Dacyczyn!
2. *Trim your food bill by 15% or more by buying the deeply discounted "loss leaders" at different stores.*

3. *Don't waste money on prepared foods.* Learn to cook from scratch for most meals.

4. *Take the farmer's market approach: buy produce when it is fresh, inexpensive, and in season* (eat it, can it, freeze it!)

5. *The highest markup items are at chest level.* This was something I had already realized intuitively when I first started using my price book. I was constantly reaching up high and getting down on my knees to pull stuff off the top and bottom shelves. The grocery stores charge a higher stocking fee ("rent") for items to be placed at chest level than for the items placed on other shelves, because most consumers shop only for things that are at eye level. When you're aware of this, it is amazing how you start looking in hidden corners for real deals.

6. *The paths to the milk and bread usually have the high-priced land mines.* (Think La Brea tar pits!) Do you think it is coincidence that the milk and bread are located in areas of the store that require the largest distances to be crossed? It shouldn't; after all, almost every family buys these items one or more times each week. Market research has been

done to get consumers to move through stores in a very specific way, past all sorts of tempting "wants" cleverly disguised as "needs."

7. *Try to shop when you're alone.* This is not always possible, but there is a financial advantage to shopping at 10 pm when the kids are at home in bed. If you aren't distracted, you can pay more attention to the true cost of items that you otherwise might just dump in the cart.

8. *Shop early in the day.* You'll be less susceptible to marketing tactics. I have also read research that recommends Monday and Tuesday as the best days to shop. (I have experienced this for myself.) The stores typically have less foot traffic on those particular days, especially in the morning.

9. *If you're hungry, eat before shopping.* I have done personal research on my family and found that we save $15 to $30 a week if we make sure we eat before walking into food stores. If I'm hungry I make sure I eat before I go.

10. *If you're tired, sleep before shopping.* I laughed out loud when I first read this "tip" because I had a five-year-old, a two-year-old, and an infant. Sleep was a long way away yet! But the rule is true. If

you are tired, you are less likely to avoid all the traps that lie in wait as you move down the aisles.

11. *Buy on markdowns at the back of the store* and save as much as 20%. Some stores have reductions as high as 40%. Is there really a difference between a loaf of bread made the same day and one that is on the day-old shelf? Only in price.

12. *Buy loss leaders.* These will help you plan the meals for the week ahead. Loss leaders are the specials that stores run to get you into the store. They are usually featured on the front and back pages of the grocery store circulars. It is infrequent that the items on "sale" on the inside pages of the circulars are really sales. But that may just be my particular area of the country. You will have to test this for yourself.

13. *Take advantage of the in-store coupon displays and the machines that spew them.* For my family this is something we rarely do. Maybe once a year. The items that have coupons are usually items that we only buy as a treat. But if you will be buying those brands on a regular basis, save a few extra cents by grabbing a coupon as you grab the item.

14. *Log onto the supermarket's online home page for more coupons.* You also will find unadvertised specials here and can get a variety of recipes and information.

15. *Seek out stores that offer double or triple coupons.* Again, for my family this is not something we do, because generic food is so much less expensive than brand-name items, even if coupon rebates are added in. But if you use brands that offer coupons, use this technique to get the most bang for your buck.

16. *Go for the triple play!* Use a manufacturer's coupon and a store's coupon on the same item.

17. *Always get a rain check* if a sale item is gone.

18. *Know when your store marks down goods that expire, like meat and bread.* The deal: use them that night or freeze them.

19. *Shop with a calculator!* This is a must. I have a zipper pocket in my price book that holds my calculator and pencils. Why is this necessary? Because in a given display, some items are sold by unit ($2.00 per can) while others are sold by weight (22¢ per ounce). You have to be able to convert the prices to a single scale on the spot, or you may miss the best deals. And I don't know about you, but I

don't do math, even simple calculations, very well in my head when my children are prancing around the aisle!

20. *Request price matching.* This is another practice that I use rarely. By visiting multiple stores I'm able to take advantage of unadvertised specials, over-stocked items that are discounted, and soon-to-expire items. One store in particular has unadvertised sales on a weekly basis, so I always go in with extra money, because I usually find one or two items on sale that are not advertised in the circulars.

21. *Always send in the rebate on a purchase.* Whether it is $2 or $50, this is 'free' money, people! Go for it. Then remember to apply the 60 / 40 principle to it when your rebate finally comes in!

22. *Bigger isn't always better in the grocery store game!* This is why your calculator is so important to have along. Marketing researchers have caught on to the fact that people are reaching for larger items thinking they will get a better deal on the price / size ratio. See point 24 (next page) for further details.

23. *Determine if buying at bulk warehouse stores is really worth your money.* We've done this three times in our family. Every time we move we have to start all over collecting data on grocery shopping because it varies radically from region to region. We have data from central New Jersey, southern California and southern Utah. We found that the warehouse stores were worth our membership rates in New Jersey and California because the stores were located nearby. However, when we moved to southern Utah the closest warehouse store was 55 miles away, and gasoline prices became a major factor in this equation (especially in the last few months!). We purchased a membership for a year and tracked prices and sales. Ultimately, we found that the membership was no longer cost-effective once the warehouse dropped the generic brand of disposable diapers from their inventory. (Yep, we use them.) That was the one item that paid for our gas. We then found that we could find products just as cheap if not cheaper in our own town when we purchased loss leaders and just stocked up.

24. *Look at "per unit" pricing.* The other day Brad went to the store to pick up dry milk and found that

if he bought the five-pound box it was actually more expensive then if he purchased the one-pound box with the ten individually sealed packets. What a waste of packaging! However, it was significantly cheaper that way – at least on this one occasion! Last year I purchased ten five-pound bags of sugar rather than one 50-pound sack because, again, the price per pound was cheaper with the five-pound bags. Crazy! Make sure you bring that calculator to the store, though, because such oddities aren't consistent. It is usually cheaper to buy in bulk, at least if you use a lot of the product!

25. *Make a shopping list before you go.* This list will not only help you remember what sales you're after, but it will decrease your time spent in the store. The longer you're in a store, the longer you're exposed to the sights, smells and sounds that retailers have been using for years to promote impulse buying. The faster you get into the store and then get out, the more money you will save since your impulse tendencies will be greatly reduced. For fun, I used to have my kids sit in the cart with a stop watch and I'd ask them to click it as

soon as we hit the first isle. It was amazing how they got into the game and even shouted at me to go faster because we were hitting the ten-minute mark.

Using All Your Resources Wisely

As you can tell by the various parts of this book, it is not only money I'm interested in using wisely. I'm an advocate for the conscious use and allocation of all your resources, including time and energy. There are simple practices that we can use in our daily lives that will contribute to our own welfare as well as to a better community.

Something as simple as the ownership of a rubber spatula for kitchen chores comes to mind. I have been in so many homes that don't own such a utensil. For me, this little 99¢ beauty saves me incredible amounts of money every day. How is that possible, you ask? Well, once again let me do the math for you. I make pancakes from scratch for my family an average of two times a week. Every time I make a batch I use my rubber spatula to scrape out the bottom and sides of the batter bowl. I am able to get a full-sized pancake each time I do this. That makes two pancakes a week that I get just by taking a few seconds to completely scrape out a bowl. This equals 104 pancakes a year! It costs me $2.24 to make a double batch of pancakes which works out to about 20 pancakes. This makes each pancake worth 11¢. Thus, the amount of money I save each year by scraping a batter bowl equals:

11¢ / pancake x 104 pancakes / year = $11.44 a year!

Multiply that by ten years and I save **$114.40**. Just for cleaning a batter bowl twice a week! When I make muffins, I usually get a full muffin from the batter bowl. However, I won't bore you with all those calculations! By the use of a rubber spatula you can save $20 to $100 a year in food that is not wasted because it was left in the container. Applesauce, peanut butter, and molasses are just a few of the items that have big returns when you're cleaning out the jars. We're not talking rocket science here, but I hope I'm showing you that the simple day-to-day food habits that you consciously engage in can alter your financial situation for better – or worse – depending upon how well you manage all your resources.

I want you to think over the other activities that you perform on a weekly or monthly basis and start adding up the savings that you can accrue by a small behavior modification. Like Linda did with the paper towels and disposable products she had purchased previously. By simply buying linen towels she's saving her family hundreds of dollars, as well as preserving a few trees for the rest of us to enjoy. The Universe is taking notes. Why shouldn't you help out as well?

Chapter 9:

The Quick-Start 10

Congratulations, you have finished the book. I'm really impressed that you read it all the way through.

To reward you for your effort and determination in finishing this tome, I'm going to give you my *Quick 10 Tips*. These simple practices will get you started on the road to wealth accumulation and financial independence today! Follow these steps with real commitment and you'll do just fine.

1.   Write your obituary, goals, and purpose statement.

2.   Track all your expenses for at least three months.

3.   Open your savings accounts (both short-term and long-term).

4.   Implement the 60 / 40 principle with your penny bank to initiate the flow of money into your life.

5.   Live within your means, always. Let nothing deter you. This is where a picture that shows your Vision will be of real help for motivation.

6.   Invest in yourself. Give early, and give often. Call three financial houses today and ask for information on investing vehicles.

7.   Declutter your house. Donate items or hold a garage sale (or throw stuff away if appropriate).

8.   Learn a new skill once a month. Make this month's skill the *Grocery Store Game.*

9.   Keep learning. Read another book on investing, or debt-free living, or wealth accumulation – and then share the principles with a friend. (See some examples in the Bibliography, on page 193)

10.   Relax! Rome wasn't built in a day. Your financial empire won't be built overnight either. We are looking for methodical, consistent

progress here. Not the boom and bust we've experienced in our own lives and see around us each day in the lives of our neighbors and nation.

Conclusion

When we lived in California, our neighbors thought we were exceptionally poor, even though our net worth and financial habits placed us solidly in the upper middle class of America. How did they get fooled?

Their assessment was based primarily on our outward behaviors. We chose to live in a modest town home next to a well landscaped but obviously industrial office complex rather than buying the overpriced suburban mansion that most of our peers selected as their version of the American dream. The neighbors saw me hanging our laundry in the garage every day and they'd ask, "Janine, why don't you just get a new dryer?" (We lived in a region in which all the dryer hookups were run on gas, and we had just purchased a brand new electric dryer about a year before the move.) I responded, "Well, the cheapest dryer I can find (that I would pay money for) is $350. There are other things I want to do with that money. So I'll hang my laundry. It is therapeutic and I like being outside. Besides, this is a desert, and it air-dries very quickly." They also saw me canning my own food (I enjoy making strawberry jam). They would see me braiding my own wool rugs for Christmas gifts. We had only one vehicle for a then family of five, and it was an older pickup truck. I would walk all the time pushing the kids in a double stroller. I walked to get groceries, to go to the library, and to buy clothes at the nearby thrift store. They would see me coming back with our purchases. The stroller would be stuffed with bags; the kids would be lugging their backpacks full of groceries and me with my backpack as well. At the time I had three children and was pregnant with number four. This was a large family for our particular block. My neighbors misinterpreted our voluntary lifestyle of frugality with quiet wealth accumulation as outright poverty! So I would have grocery bags anonymously left on my doorstep. This is no lie. There were bags left at least once a week of clothes, toys for the kids, and food.

When we got ready to leave for Utah, my neighbors were astounded. They asked us, "Where are you going?" We said that we were relocating and that we had a house picked out. It just blew their minds. "How can you afford it?" was a common question. They sent a collection through the neighborhood to help us with our moving expenses! I cried when I got the money. I cried for two reasons. I'm not normally an emotional person, but I was so grateful, because I knew where that money came from, and the sacrifices required by our neighbors in making this farewell gift. It was the 60 / 40 principle at work in our lives. I also cried because they didn't understand our real situation, that we were moving as the result of a carefully planned and vigilantly executed fiscal program. I didn't know how to tell them that financial independence doesn't just have to be a dream. Even those of us on a regular salary can achieve this goal – if we choose to do so, and spend the necessary time and energy to see the commitment through.

That is why I am grateful that you have given me your reading time so that I could discuss this topic with you. It is my dream that you will become a wealth accumulator, too, and enjoy the financial peace that permeates your life when you are debt-free and exercising the good habits that lead to financial independence. Make the choice today. Do it for yourself, for your future, and for the country. Money isn't just for the rich. Wealth is for all of us – if we elect to make it ours.

Appendix I:

Can This Data Be Any More Skewed?

These data are derived from the financial efforts of participants from a financial independence seminar that I gave in November of 2004, consisting of 135 attendees at the George Wythe College President's Forum. Students, alumni and friends of the college were invited to this presentation for free or at minimal cost (paid to the college). The seminar was scheduled over a day and a half period with the President of the college, Dr. Oliver DeMille, giving two keynote talks, one at the beginning of the session and one at the conclusion. Dr. Brad Bolon (that's right, my Brad) spoke for an hour during the second day on investing options. (This book is already too long to include his information here, but we'll delve into this topic more fully in forthcoming volumes.) Each participant received bound copies of the seminar notes and worksheets for the Grocery Store Game (Appendix III, page 188). Upon conclusion of the seminar, participants were handed survey forms that gave them the opportunity to volunteer for three months of free telephone mentoring in exchange for permission to use their financial data (anonymously, of course!).

The goal of this experiment was to determine whether or not the habits needed for successful wealth accumulation could be established in such a short time as three months. My actual hypothesis was that a good financial education would motivate almost all individuals to *get started today*. Wealth accumulation was defined as a seminar participant who was able to increasingly save money over the three months of the study; participants were asked to provide balances of short- and long-term savings accounts, and had to demonstrate an increase in the long-term savings balances over time in order to be considered a success. The long-term savings vehicle was proposed to be the biggest indicator of wealth accumulating tendencies, as the changes in the amounts in this account would show if the flow of money was intact or had been broken. How? Because only contributions to such long-term vehicles represent a real measure of a commitment to wealth accumulation, as they cannot be withdrawn easily for use in short-term consumption.

When a scientist is working on an experiment dealing with behavior, she tries to normalize the data by picking random segments of the population base to control strongly for the variables that she knows will influence the data and bias the ultimate interpretation. I had no such luck with this population, as all but one person was a member of the Church of Jesus Christ of Latter Day Saints, and almost half had already started to address their financial shortcomings on their own.

Of the 135 attendees at the President's Forum, 113 individuals signed up for telephone mentoring. Each mentoring call lasted an average of 28.9 minutes (with a maximum of 30 minutes allocated per call). Calls were placed at two weeks after the seminar, four weeks after the first phone call, and six weeks after the second phone call. Of the 113 people who signed up for mentoring, 38 (34%) dropped from the study or made themselves ineligible (by not doing the homework activities [complete an obituary, track expenses, cut up all but one credit card, and write a purpose statement]) after the first phone call. The remaining 75 participants included 33 families and nine single students.

The average age of the 75 participants was 35.2 years, their average gross income was $47,098, and the mean family size was five. Most participants (59, or 79%) were located in Utah, with five (12%) from Nevada and four (9%) from California. Before the seminar, the average participant's savings account held $5,812, but 45% of them had saved $500 or less. This savings was typically held in a short-term savings account; 24 (73%) of the 33 families but none of the students had retirement accounts in place. The mean total debt load for the population was $204,969 with credit card debt averaging $5,099 and car loans averaging $6,216. The average debt on the primary home was $157,484 for the 67% of people who were home owners; the remaining 33% (including all students) were renters. Other sources of debt such as school loans, medical bills, loans from family and other loans averaged $36,169 per family, with 14% coming from second mortgages. Before the seminar, 50% of the participants owed nothing on their vehicle(s), and 57% had no credit card debt.

After completing three months of mentoring, 95% of the participants (31 of 33 families and all the students) had developed the habits that promote wealth accumulation. After attending the seminar and being mentored, the average wealth accumulator's savings account had increased to $8,609 (up by 48%), with increases recorded in both short-term and long-term savings vehicles. More importantly, the 45% of people who had saved $500 or less before the program now had savings account balances of $1,044 (an increase of at least 109%)! Of all the participants who had received the classroom experience and intensive follow-up coaching, only two families chose not to become wealth accumulators in the 3-month period.

Bottom line? I proved my hypothesis. Almost all the participants who completed the program increased their total savings by 50% or more in only three months. That is my definition of success!

Appendix II:

A Word on Philanthropy to My Spiritually Minded Friends

You will recall that Philanthropy, the donation of a 10% portion of your income, is a major pillar of the money cycle that forms the road to financial independence.

Interestingly, I find that this concept is understood more readily by my clients that have no formal spiritual affiliation. I expect that this is true because, lacking the obligation to make a division of their contributions between competing church and secular charities, they can just select a single entity and give.

On the other hand, my spiritually minded clients had trouble comprehending the principle of true philanthropy. I will illustrate this point using my November, 2004 seminar as an example.

Out of the 75 individuals involved in this study, only one person (1.3% of the participants) was not a member of one specific sect, the Church of Jesus Christ of Latter Day Saints (LDS). My follow up phone mentoring with these people indicated that the philanthropic element was frequently broken by my 74 LDS participants due to certain charitable options available to the LDS membership. (Remember, it is not the nature or value of these funds that is in dispute, merely their relation to the philanthropic arm in the flow of money into your life.)

Whenever an LDS member told me that money had stopped flowing in their life (demonstrated by a sudden need to pull money from savings), I would ask them where their philanthropic moneys were going. I learned of five major philanthropic destinations from these participants and quickly found that three of the five would break the flow of money if the 10% dedicated to philanthropy was given to them. The five funds in question are:

1. Fast Offering Fund
2. Humanitarian Aid Fund
3. Missionary Aid Fund
4. Book of Mormon Fund
5. Perpetual Education Fund

The first two funds, Fast Offering and Humanitarian Aid, are just fine for philanthropy. These funds "take care of thy neighbor" by pooling resources and assisting either local church members or giving assistance internationally. Thus, these two are totally appropriate places to ship the 10% of your income that you designate for philanthropy.

In contrast, the last three funds will cause problems to your wealth accumulation efforts, and appear to do so for differing reasons. The Missionary Aid Fund and the Book of Mormon Fund are part of "taking care of God's Church." This effort is already supported by you through the 10% tithe to the church. The Perpetual Education Fund works a bit differently. When money is donated to this fund, it is put into a financial repository for recipients to receive student loans for continuing education. However, the recipients of this money are required to pay it back once they have completed their educations. This causes the money to fold back onto itself and will break the flow of money from external sources.

I strongly encouraged the LDS participants that I mentored by phone not to give their 10% philanthropic segment to the last three funds. I recommend this not because these are unworthy, but because contributions to these in lieu of real philanthropic gifts will prevent you from becoming a true wealth accumulator. If you feel "prompted" to give to these funds, by all means do so. Just make sure that the donations to these three causes come out of your 60% Living allotment or 10% tithe. In all cases, when the philanthropic segment was redirected, the flow of money returned to the participant's life.

The same traps may await those of you from other sects with many different opportunities to donate to good causes sponsored by your own spiritual organization. So what is the bottom line? In selecting your charities, be sure to clarify the nature of the fund to which you are sending your money. In my experience, if the contributions will benefit church members only or serve only to proselytize others, that need falls under the "Tithe" arm or the "Living" arm of the money star. You will need to look for ways to truly spread your gifts of money outside your own family, spiritual as well as blood relations.

Appendix III:

The Grocery Store Game

The Grocery Store Game may be the quickest and easiest way to reduce expenses and prove to yourself that the principles of wealth accumulation that I have outlined in this book will actually work for you.

Each participant at the President's Forum was given a three-ring binder with two pages of suggestions for making their grocery shopping more productive. The binder also included a transparent vinyl page for holding business cards in which they were encouraged to store their club cards and shopping cards, a translucent vinyl pocket page in which to keep their circulars and shopping lists, an A to Z index to facilitate filing the entries for their frequently purchased items, and a sample page from my price book.

I found that most participants resisted implementing this tool at first, especially those from families who thought themselves already quite frugal with their grocery shopping. I challenged these particular people to prove me wrong by using the tool for a short time. Upon actually trying the system, all the participants started to use it weekly. I received many comments on how much money the system saved them despite the fact that they believed me unable to teach them anything new about savvy shopping.

I encourage you to emulate these skeptics and discover the power of this technique in your own life by undertaking the same experiment for yourself. Remember, every little bit helps – and this tool will save you hundreds or even thousands of dollars a year, starting immediately!

Appendix IV: Glossary

Burn Rate – The average amount of money that a household spends per month (i.e., expenses).

Charity – Any service, item or money given away or donated.

Consumer / Consume – To destroy, to use up, to squander, to devour, to spend wastefully.

Conserver / Conserve – To keep from being damaged, lost, or wasted; to save.

Financial Independence – Having enough regular income to meet living expenses from a source other than paid employment.

Philanthropy – Money that is given away to a non-family member. It is even more powerful if given anonymously.

Wealth Accumulator – A person who follows the 60 / 40 principle consistently for life. (Another definition I developed from the positive experiences of my seminar participants was: a person who followed the 60 / 40 principle for three months and saw a progressive increase in their long-term savings account.)

Appendix V:

The Author's Biography

Any time you read a "get rich quick" or even a "get rich slow" book, it's only fair that you have a chance to find out something about the quack who authored the tome.

I love the challenge of starting a business from a simple idea and watching it morph into a money-making venture serving the needs of my community (social entrepreneurship). I began my training in frugal living as an entrepreneur starting at age 10. The first business I created for myself was bagging groceries at the local commissary for tips. By age 15 I had cycled through a series of successful businesses, each of which I sold for a profit. The last one I had before college was a cleaning firm (I chatted with Sam Walton while running this one [page 42]); I sold its client list before heading to the University of Missouri at Columbia to pursue a degree in Biochemistry. I took five years to get my Bachelor in Science degree because I put myself through school. I did this by working two and three jobs at a time as well as by selling my horse, car and stereo; no time for running a business at school! Upon graduation I had accrued a debt of only $1,700 (all in student loans for the last year).

I married my husband, Brad, during my last year of college, after which we began a series of moves around the country to further his education and take ever-higher paying jobs. I worked as a biochemist in university laboratories for seven years and then moved into corporate pharmaceutical research for eight years. Along the way, I started two businesses (only one of which succeeded) before having the joy of motherhood thrust upon me.

Since moving to Utah, my husband and I have both undertaken graduate degrees and have both started part-time consulting businesses that we run together from our home. We have spawned four children along the way (currently ages 8, 6, 3, and 2) who we have chosen to home school. As with each of us, I'm always too busy, but I have always enjoyed being an entrepreneur and am thrilled that I can now move into the ranks of a social entrepreneur by founding SmartCents, Inc. It's a real pleasure to use this business to give back, not only in money but in time.

Appendix VI:

Annotated Bibliography

I have included this short list of books for you as a quick means to find those three good volumes with which to jumpstart your new life and self-education in wealth accumulation and financial independence. I have given my opinions on their value to me, but you will have to judge for yourself their worth to you. Happy reading!

Aslett, Don; *Clutter's Last Stand* **and** *Not for Packrats Only;* 1984

A good friend said to me, "Janine, you're doing these financial seminars, you've mentored me for awhile, and you've got to talk about clutter." I think Aslett does a much better job talking about clutter than I ever will. He runs several cleaning companies; I immediately fell in love with these books because I put myself through school by cleaning homes. My first reaction after reading his books was, "Where were his books when I was doing this?" I would have done my job faster and more efficiently using his methods. His style is light and humorous, and I enjoyed the line art that he used to drive his points home. It is a fast read as well as powerful. Most importantly, the connection between too much stuff and poor financial habits is real, and Aslett's philosophy will help you to break the chain on this end.

Avanzini, John; *30, 60, Hundred Fold: Your Financial Harvest Released*; 1989

I recommend that you get this out-of-print book from the library. The last two chapters are the most powerful; however, you have to read the whole book to understand why the last two chapters have such punch. Avanzini talks about how our moving from an agrarian society to an industrial one cost us our understanding of how money grows. It is an excellent description on how the Universe handles philanthropy. He uses the analogy of the farmer and a field of wheat. It is a fascinating story showing us how we've lost our understanding of money since we no longer grow our own food. Avanzini is a Baptist minister and there are frequent scriptural references. If you're not a Christian, you will find yourself skimming through a lot of it, but the financial principles are sound.

Bach, David; *The Automatic Millionaire*; 2004

Bach is a financial planner and calls upon an interesting couple that came to him for advice on financial independence. Their story, which is the basis of the book, tells how *they taught him* to become wealthy. This book is a fast read and gives many excellent pointers on how to make your wealth accumulation program automatic. In my experience, the less you have to think about it and make adjustments, the better off you'll be.

Dacyczyn, Amy; *The Tightwad Gazette* (three volumes), 1995

I recommend that anybody who wants to truly learn frugality, even if you already think that you're frugal, buy this book. Dacyczyn (pronounced "decision") is incredible when it comes to saving money. I guarantee that you will learn something.

Dominguez, Joe and Robin, Vicki; *Your Money or Your Life*; 1999

The authors of this book do a wonderful job of assisting you to work through the emotions that distort your view of money. I use this book all the time in my seminars, and believe that the principles described here are pivotal in assisting people to get out of debt and become financially free. Brad and I suggest that you take the advice on investing (buy bonds and nothing else) with a truckload of salt. When the book was first written in the 1970s, bonds were commanding a hefty 13% return!

Harris, Blaine & Coonradt, Charles, *The Four Laws of Debt-Free Prosperity*, 1996

This is a great refresher book. It is one man's walk from a heavy debt load to financial peace with the guidance of a kindly neighbor. I like the style of it since it is told in story form, and I enjoyed the witty tit-for-tat between the main character, Paul, and his wealthy neighbor, Mary.

Hunt, Mary; *The Complete Cheapskate*, 2003

This book is excellent if you have credit card debt. It will help you work through addictive behaviors that are not in your best interest if you are a wealth accumulator wanna-be.

King, Dean; *The Penny Pincher's Almanac Handbook for Modern Frugality*; 1992

This is a small book, but it packs punch! There are hundreds of simple ways to save yourself money. Some of the topics discussed are shopping strategies, food, home, appliances, utilities, clothing, automobiles, health, money management, education, and enjoying the life you're leading.

Kiyosaki, Robert; *Rich Dad, Poor Dad*; 1998
Once you have learned to live within your means and you
have all your credit card debts paid off, this is a great book
to start learning how to double your income. This will help
you to the next phase of wealth accumulation. Keep in
mind that the principles will apply even if you choose
something other than real estate (the route that Kiyosaki
advocates for building wealth) as your avenue of increasing
your income.

Long, Charles, *How to Live Without a Salary*, 1980
I enjoy Long's laid-back view on life and his ability to
haggle. I learned the art of barter through this book and
how to think through what I thought I needed versus what I
really needed. You'll find his real life examples charming
and informative.

Orman, Suze; *The 9 Steps to Financial Freedom*; 1997
Orman is a certified financial planner who spent a good
part of this book discussing attitudes about money and how
we hurt our financial future by not addressing them. I liked
her practical approach to investments, and estate and
retirement planning. When you are ready to invest, this is a
good book to start you on your way to being your own best
financial councilor.

Stanley, Thomas & Danko, William; *The Millionaire
Next Door*; 1996
I recommend this book if you think you're alone in your
goals. You'll find out how real millionaires live. If you
want to learn more about the lifestyle, this is the book for
you. The research Stanley and Danko have done is eye
opening as they asked 385 real but "ordinary" millionaires
about their lifestyles, how they spend their money and what
they really like to do for leisure. If you aspire to financial

independence, this book provides a great roadmap for the habits of successful wealth accumulators.

Stanley, Thomas; *The Millionaire Women Next Door*; 2004
Stanley continued his research and came up with a sample population of 233 women who had a net worth over $1 million or more. He then discussed the difference between millionaire women and men as well as the attitudes that others had about these two different populations. Again, a good discussion of the habits used by real-life wealth accumulators.

Index

Notes

(Can you read a book without taking notes? I can't! So I added a
few pages for those who like to doodle while they read.)